Hudson Taylor

Living Water

Hudson Taylor

Living Water

Rod Thomson

CLC
PUBLICATIONS

Hudson Taylor: Living Water
Published by CLC Publications

U.S.A.
P.O. Box 1449, Fort Washington, PA 19034

GREAT BRITAIN
51 The Dean, Alresford, Hants. SO24 9BJ

This edition 2012

Printed in the United States of America

ISBN-10 (mass market): 1-61958-023-3
ISBN-13 (mass market): 978-1-61958-023-7

Contents

1

To the Heart of the Matter

Hudson Taylor had led the earnest Chinese merchant to faith in Jesus only days earlier. Hoping to find peace, Mr. Nyi had examined several other religions in vain but now was filled with joy at the salvation offered by Jesus. He was already telling his friends about Jesus and almost overnight turning into a preacher of the gospel. Quite unexpectedly, Nyi asked Taylor a question that pierced the young missionary from London with guilt and sadness:

"How long have you had the Glad Tidings in England?" he asked his face beaming the joy he had just found.

Taylor was ashamed and responded vaguely, "Oh, several hundred years, maybe." He avoided eye contact at that moment.

"What! Several hundred years!" Nyi exclaimed. "Is it possible that you have known about Jesus for so long and only now have come to tell us?"

Taylor was silent. Nyi went on.

"My father sought the truth for more than twenty years and died without finding it. Oh, why did you not come sooner?"

There was no answer Hudson Taylor could give. He felt a sense of personal guilt at this charge. But even more deeply, it stirred in him the desire to spread the good news of the gospel of Jesus Christ to the hundreds of millions of Chinese who lived in darkness not knowing the Light of the world.

"Then go, for Me, to China." Those were the words God had stamped on his heart in answer to prayer. It was a lifelong calling. The burden was heavy on his heart from his youth until his death. Nyi's comments reinforced the importance and the urgency.

There were a few missionaries in the coastal cities of China. These were cities controlled partly by the British. They were called "treaty ports" because foreigners were permitted to live there under a treaty between the British and the Chinese governments. But in the vast interior of the Chinese nation, where most of the people lived, foreigners were not allowed. No missionaries could travel there to spread the Light. Those people did not know that God had come to earth as a man and died on a cross more than eighteen hundred years earlier so that their sins could be erased forever.

They had never even heard of Jesus.

Instead, they believed in many false religions, such as Buddhism and Confucianism and Taoism. Those beliefs were as unfulfilling for most Chinese as they were for Nyi and his father. They could promise no eternal safety or knowledge of the one true God.

Hudson Taylor ached for the millions of Chinese who were dying without any knowledge of God's grace. He longed with all his heart to tell them about the death and resurrection of Jesus so that they might live with peace and joy, knowing that when they died, they would be immediately in the presence of the Savior, rejoicing in heaven.

He committed every aspect of his life completely to service for the Lord. It would cost him the lives of three of his children and of his dear wife. It would cost him his health, as he endured many diseases and injuries. And it would mean learning the hard way to trust in God to meet every financial need that he and his fellow missionaries had.

However, Hudson Taylor's life was not one of heartache but of a deep and abiding love for the Lord. It was filled with joy. The sacrifices he made in his devotion to evangelizing the Chinese were great but the reward was greater, both for him and for the Chinese people. For the Chinese it meant tens of thousands of lives brought into the light of Jesus Christ—the beginning of an impact that continues today. For Hudson Taylor it meant learning a deep lesson through his hard trials—that God's grace truly is sufficient for any need.

"Whoever drinks of the water that I shall give him will never thirst" (John 4:14). It was true!

2

The Finished Work Begins

A very young James Hudson Taylor sat at the dinner table while his mother busily attended to guests. In fact, she was so busy serving that she completely overlooked her little boy's plate, which sat empty in front of him. The Taylor children were taught not to ask for things at the table, but instead to wait until the food was offered.

So he sat silently, waiting. The meal went on for a long time while little Hudson waited patiently. Then he had an idea. He asked that the salt be passed,

One of the guests, noticing that the boy's plate was empty, asked: "And what do you want the salt for?"

"Oh, I want to be ready," was the confident reply. "Mamma will give me something to eat by and by."

Such simple faith was a cornerstone of the Taylor household.

James Hudson Taylor was born on May 21, 1832, in Barnsley, Yorkshire, England, and never lacked the Word of God as a child. Named after his father's first name, James, and his mother's family name, Hudson, he was continually surrounded by the gospel and the rules for living that it set forth.

He was the only son of James and Amelia Taylor.

His father was a pharmacist and a Methodist lay preacher. James Taylor taught and preached about God. He was not ordained as a minister of a church, but he gave sermons at many different churches. Twice daily he held family worship, making God a central part of his children's lives. He also gave the children practical lessons in making the Scripture real in their lives.

Prayer and Bible study were considered so important that each child was allotted at least a half hour per day just for that.

Father Taylor was very strict and taught his children a disciplined lifestyle of structured daily living and duty. One outstanding character trait he taught the children, which would be important for his son in later years, was self-control.

The children were to be punctual by making sure they were on time for meals. Nor were they allowed to dally while dressing. And if there was a chore to be done, it should be tackled immediately.

There was also basic self-denial.

"See if you can do without," he would say, particularly to the pleasures of eating. "By and by, you will have to say no to yourself when we are not there to help you; and you will find it very difficult when you want a thing tremendously. So let us try to practice now, for the sooner you begin, the stronger will be the habit."

This practical teaching of self-control and self-denial was a valuable part of Hudson Taylor's makeup when he was in poverty on the mission trail.

His father also was very honest and careful with money, making it a point to pay every bill owed by the day it was due. He used to say that if he let it go even a week, the person he owed the money to was losing a little bit of interest on it.

His mother's gentle discipline and her teaching of history and geography were also important factors in his growing years. She kept an orderly house—just as her son would keep all his affairs in good order for the Lord's work.

Because of his father's role in the church, the family often entertained visiting ministers. A constant topic of conversation was foreign missions. The vast country of China was foremost in James Taylor's heart. It bothered him that his church did nothing for the Chinese.

"Why do we not send missionaries there?" he would lament. "That is the country to aim at, with its teeming population, its strong, intelligent, scholarly people."

Little Hudson Taylor picked up his father's fervor for China. He read and reread a small book called *China* in the family's well-organized library, until he practically had it memorized. He was on fire with the idea.

"Father, why don't we send Christians to China?"

James Taylor set his teacup down on its saucer with a clink and looked at his small, earnest son.

"Well, Son, there are many difficulties. The Chinese don't really want foreigners in their land. That makes it hard."

"Have we tried?"

"Oh, yes, I suppose. There are some Englishmen there telling people about Jesus. But just a few in the big ports. There is such a need, so many people . . ." His father's voice trailed off as he picked up his teacup and sipped again, looking past the wall of books in the library.

Little Hudson frowned and thought for a moment. Then he perked up.

"I want to go to China, when I become a man, so that the Chinese can become Christians!" he exclaimed.

His father broke from his thoughts and looked back at the shining face of his son—his sickly, frail son—and smiled lovingly at him.

"Nothing is too difficult for God. But you do not seem to have been created for the harsh life of a missionary in a faraway country like China. You need to be strong and healthy to survive in such a land."

"But I might be stronger when I am older," Hudson suggested hopefully.

The elder Taylor sighed.

"Perhaps, Son. But do not be disappointed if it is not God's will."

Nonetheless, Hudson Taylor had his mind set upon China at a very young age.

Seeing their son go abroad as a missionary would have been a joy to James and Amelia, but they were acutely aware of his recurring ailments. Hudson was not sent off to school until he was eleven years old. Even then, he would miss a day or two every week because of illness. Because of his small size, combined with his sickly nature, he had few friends among the sports-minded boys at the school. After only two years, his parents brought him home, and he spent the rest of his youth being taught at home by his parents and working with his father.

A future as a missionary to China seemed like a daydream.

At seventeen years of age, Hudson faced the biggest spiritual crisis of his life to that point. On the outside he was a bright Christian teen with few cares; on the inside, however, he was falling into rebellion and unbelief.

It began when he went to work as a junior clerk at a Barnsley bank, where most of the young men he worked with were not believers. Rather, they were full of the world and openly mocked Christians. A particularly popular, handsome, slightly older clerk never missed a chance to tease Hudson. The fellow took nothing seriously and tried to influence Hudson in the same direction.

"Such old-fashioned notions!" he exclaimed after overhearing Hudson tell another worker about God's offer of salvation. "You would think that in this day and age no one would still be buying such ancient myths." The year was 1849.

"The Bible is not about myths," Hudson answered quietly, continuing to count receipts.

The young man gave him a condescending smirk. "Fairy tales and silliness. A man living in a fish. All the animals fitting on a boat. The sea parting in two. C'mon. You can't prove one ounce of it. And you're a fool to believe it."

Hudson didn't look at the man. "I know what is in my heart, and what is true, by faith—and it is Jesus. Just because you can't see Him doesn't mean He is not real."

The young man scoffed.

"What is real is that it is time for us to go hunting," he said, closing his ledger, grabbing his coat and heading out the door. "You go read your Bible," he shouted back with a laugh. It was about the last thing Hudson planned to do.

The daily drumming of these companions wore him down. He began to long for the superficial, self-entertaining distractions of the others. He wanted to participate in parties, meet girls, have money and buy a horse for hunting. Keeping up the outward appearance of Christianity became harder.

After a few months his eyes became inflamed because of night work by gaslight, and he had to resign from the bank and return to work with his father. But his struggles with wanting immediate gratification continued. His typically bright attitude toward things became more and more cloudy, and it showed in the household.

His father wanted to help him, but the elder Taylor's skills were not well suited to this phase of his son's life. His patience with Hudson wore thin.

His mother had a better grasp of Hudson's troubles and was patient and prayerful for her son.

But it was Amelia, his thirteen-year-old sister, whom he was closest to. He could talk freely to her. They had a special confidence in each other that would last a lifetime. His unhappy state probably affected her even more than it did his parents. So she finally decided to pray for him three times daily until he was truly converted to faith in Christ. She was faithful in doing this for many days, making notes in her journal. With the prayers going up all around him from those who loved him best, he came to the spiritual turning point in his life.

While his parents were gone because his father was preaching about seventy miles away, and Hudson was on holiday, he looked through his father's library for a book. Finding nothing with which to while away the time, he sorted through a basket of pamphlets and pulled out a gospel tract that looked interesting. He figured, *There will be a story at the beginning and a sermon at the end, so I'll just read the beginning.*

He sat down with a lightsome attitude and no thought of salvation. That was not the case seventy miles away, where his mother was deep in prayer for the conversion of her only son. She went alone into the room where they were staying, locked the door and determined to stay on her knees until she knew for sure that her prayers were answered. Hour after hour she pleaded for her son. Although she was exhausted, she prayed until she knew by the Holy Spirit that God had answered her prayers and converted her son.

Meanwhile, back home, Hudson was reading the pamphlet and came across the phrase "the finished work of Christ."

What does the author mean by that? Why not say the "atoning" work?

Immediately the words came to his mind: "It is finished."

What is finished?

And then it came to his mind and heart like a light flashing: "A full and perfect atonement and satisfaction for sin. The whole debt was paid for our sins, and not for ours only, but for the sins of the whole world."

So if the whole work is finished and the whole debt paid, what is there left for me to do? he asked. Suddenly there dawned a joyful understanding from the Holy Spirit. There is nothing for me to do but fall down on my knees, accept Jesus as Savior and praise Him forever.

And at that moment Hudson Taylor joyously praised the Lord for his salvation, and his mother knew in her heart, seventy miles away, that her prayers were answered.

He told only Amelia what had happened and made her promise not to tell anyone else. Several days later his parents returned home, and he met his mother at the door, spilling the good news to her.

She wrapped her arms around him. "I know, my boy."

"Why," he asked in surprise, "has Amelia broken her promise? She said she would tell no one."

His mother assured him that it was not Amelia or any other human who had told her. The power of prayer became very real to Hudson at that moment. It was reinforced when he inadvertently came upon his sister's pocketbook journal that he mistook for his own and saw the promise to pray for him three times daily until he was saved. That was one month before God brought him from darkness into light.

From June 1849 onward Hudson Taylor never wavered in his faith in Christ or God's promise to answer prayers. He came to rely on that promise more and more as God's plan for him unfolded.

3

Preparing for the Great Call

The change in Hudson Taylor was dramatic. He delighted in studying the Bible and in prayer time. The years of Christian discipline at home paid off, because there were very few worldly habits that had to be dealt with. He and Amelia began a campaign of passing out tracts and caring for others in the poorest parts of Barnsley every Sunday afternoon.

But Hudson continued to struggle with the sin he knew to be in him. He still lacked something. He wrestled with a continual backsliding spirit that he longed to be rid of. It saddened him that he could not act always in a way that was pleasing to God. One day, when he was struggling mightily with this, he clung to the Lord in prayer. A promise welled up in him: If God would break the power of sin in his life and give him freedom from it, he would renounce earthly desires and do whatever God directed him to.

"I felt I was in the presence of God, entering into a covenant with the Almighty. I felt as though I wished to withdraw my promise, but could not. Something seemed to say, 'Your prayer is answered, your conditions are accepted.' And from that time the conviction never left me that I was called to China."

What he heard distinctly, as if from the very mouth of God, was: "Then go, for Me, to China."

The whole experience gave a very specific meaning to Hudson Taylor's life. All of his pursuits and studies turned to this God-given plan to take the gospel to the Chinese. The things of the world that had continued to tempt him began to fade.

Hudson tried to learn everything he could about China. He even obtained a copy of the Gospel of Luke in the Chinese language from a Christian brother connected with the British and Foreign Bible Society. While the man agreed to lend him the book, he admonished Taylor—saying that when he grew older he would become wise enough to know that he could not be a missionary to China.

He did what he could with this tiny bit of help and was able to pick up some portions of the language in its written form. But he did not know how to pronounce the strange symbols.

He continued to learn about dispensing medicine by observing his father's work. But it was time for him to take a step that would prove a valuable asset in China—learning medicine.

At age nineteen he went to Hull and began work as an assistant to a relative, Dr. Robert Hardey. The kind doctor taught him the basics of medicine and treating the sick, skills that Taylor would use extensively to show his goodwill to the Chinese and provide an open door for the gospel.

But Satan kept buffeting.

Hudson met a missionary while visiting London, who warned him about going to China.

"Are you not aware that the Chinese look very different from you? You have blond hair, blue eyes and fair skin—very much an Englishman! But they have black hair and dark eyes, and darker skin."

"I know," Taylor said quietly but firmly, although he had never actually seen a Chinese person.

The missionary pressed his point.

"You will never do for China. They call me a red-haired devil; they would run from you in terror! You could never get them to listen," he said. Taylor accepted the older man's words of experience and did not argue with him. After all, here was a man who had lived in China. Even so, he remained confident of his calling.

It is God who called me, and He knew all the time about the color of my hair and eyes, he thought to himself. *No, God knows what He is doing, sending someone who looks like me to the Chinese! Perhaps my looks won't count for as much as my actions,* he mused.

He learned a lesson more valuable than medicine while working for Dr. Hardey; he learned to rely on God to supply all of his needs. The doctor was a good man, but he was very busy dealing with sick people. Side issues, such as Taylor's monthly pay, seemed to get lost in his schedule. The doctor asked Taylor to remind him when his pay was due. But Taylor resolved not to ask the doctor for the money, even when it was overdue. Instead, he chose to ask his heavenly Father who promised to provide all his needs.

"If I cannot rely on God while in England with friends and family, how will I be able to rely on Him among the Chinese? When I get to China, I will have no claim on anyone for anything. My only claim will be on God. I must learn to rely on God and to move other men solely through the power of prayer."

God was ready to hone this lesson to a fine edge.

One particular time the money owed him was far overdue, and he was nearly penniless.

The payment date had come and gone, and Taylor kept praying daily, asking God to remind Dr. Hardey of the money due. The days past due turned into weeks past due. When Taylor tallied his finances, he found he had about enough for one more meal—then every last cent would be gone.

While visiting a lodging house for poor people that night, he had his last coin with him—enough for breakfast the next day. One of the men to whom he had just relayed the gospel had a sick wife and asked Taylor to come to his home and pray for her. On the way there the man told him they were starving, and he was not sure how long his wife would last. Taylor thought of the single coin in his pocket. *If only it was several smaller coins, I would split them with the man*, he thought.

At the poor man's home, he prayed and told of the love of God. But his heart was heavy, and he began feeling like a hypocrite for not giving them anything of substance, while telling them of the care of the Lord.

"You can see what a terrible state we are in," the man pleaded. "If there is anything you can do for us, please do so."

The despair was clear to Taylor. But he had so little. Then the verse came to mind: "Give to him that asketh thee."

He reached in his pocket and took out the coin and placed it in the man's hand.

"It may not seem like much, seeing that I am comparatively well off, but in parting with that coin, I am giving you my all," Taylor told him. "What I am telling you is true; God really is the Father and can be trusted."

The man squeezed the coin in his hand. "Oh, thank you, sir. You have saved us," he said with tears in his eyes.

In giving the money, a great joy flooded Hudson Taylor's heart. He returned home, now without means for breakfast in the morning but fully confident that the Father would provide for His child.

Early the next morning, the landlady knocked on his door with an envelope in her wet hand. He looked at the handwriting but did not recognize it. And the postmark had been smudged by the landlady. The envelope had no letter in it, only a blank piece of paper folded over a pair of child's gloves. But out of the gloves fell a large coin worth four times more than the coin he had given away the night before.

"Praise the Lord!" he exclaimed out loud. "A 400 percent return for twelve hours' investment—that is good interest!"

The anonymous gift was an important lesson in God's everlasting care, an event that he looked back on many times for comfort from life's storms.

In 1852 Taylor moved to London to further his medical training and to get in close contact with the Chinese Evangelization Society, which he had heard about in Hull. He stayed in a boarding house with his uncle, Benjamin Hudson, and a cousin. While they were family and happy to share their apartment, they were not Christians and so gave him a hard time about his faith at times. But he had been down this road of testing before and was ready with a defense this time.

More trying was the disorganization at the Chinese Evangelization Society. He had been in written contact with the Society, and they had told him that they would help put him through his medical training at the hospital. But when he arrived in London, he found that nothing had been done. It was a disorganization that would plague him for years.

Taylor was growing closer to God and learning to trust in Him alone. So he took all these matters and more to the Father, who came through faithfully for him. Soon he was working in the hospital.

Knowing the hardships that would face him in China, Taylor determined to learn to live as simply and cheaply as possible. He wanted to be physically, emotionally and spiritually ready. He walked the several miles to the hospital to avoid the cost of transportation, lived on brown bread, apples and water for long periods of time. But he became sick while working at the hospital. Deathly sick.

Shortly after doing some dissecting work on the body of a man who had died of a serious fever, he began feeling faint and sick. By late afternoon he was feeling much worse, and his arms and legs ached. He realized he had to return to the apartment. As he put away his apparatus, he explained the symptoms to a nearby surgeon.

"I cannot think what has come over me," he said. But it was clear to the experienced doctor.

"Why, what has happened is clear enough," said the surgeon. "You must have cut yourself while dissecting, and this is a case of malignant fever."

Immediately, Taylor remembered how he had cut himself the night before with a needle but then forgotten about it. The surgeon, who had seen many cases of the deadly fever, told Taylor to go straight home.

"Get all your affairs in order," the doctor said. "For you are a dead man."

So focused was he on his missionary calling that Hudson Taylor's first thoughts were sorrow that he would never be able to go to China. Yet he took that terrible moment to witness to the surgeon.

"There is a joy in thinking that I will soon see my Master and Savior. Yet I don't think I will die, because I have work to do in China."

The surgeon was a confirmed skeptic, but he must have been touched by such a deep faith at that moment.

And God was true to His calling of Hudson Taylor. After weeks of bedridden sickness, he slowly recovered his health and some strength. His uncle supplied him with every need. When he was strong enough, he returned home for further rest and healing.

He was fully healthy—as fully healthy as Hudson Taylor ever became—and waiting on God for the next step, when he received a letter from the Chinese Evangelization Society in London. They offered him the opportunity to be a missionary to China for their organization.

On June 4, 1853, Hudson Taylor accepted the offer, and on September 19, at the young age of twenty-one, he was at the port of Liverpool, preparing to leave. It was a relatively small, double-masted sailing ship carrying cargo and one passenger.

Taylor's mother was there to see him off. She boarded the ship and went with him to his tiny cabin in the hull. She lovingly smoothed the bed and sat down next to him. They sang a hymn and prayed together and hugged. Then the captain called out for them to separate. His mother controlled her feelings and walked off the ship. Standing on the dock, she looked up to see her only son standing on the deck, looking at her. They both assumed they would not see each other again on earth.

Suddenly, she could control her emotions no longer, and a cry of anguish shot out of her, cutting through her son like a knife. At that moment he had a fuller understanding of the verse, "For God so loved the world, that he gave his only begotten son . . ."

Then the ship pulled away from the pier. Hudson Taylor, full of love for God and aching to tell the Chinese about the Savior, began a six-month voyage to Shanghai, China.

The missionary world would never be the same.

4

China!

Shanghai is an ancient Chinese city on the shore of the Pacific. During the height of the British Empire, it had a small European community under the protection of the British government. The harbor brought in trade and some travelers. The narrow streets were typical of Chinese cities, almost covered with wooden signs and awnings blocking out much of the sky. Mostly, it teemed with Chinese in their traditional pajama-like garb.

When Hudson Taylor arrived in China on March 1, 1854, the country was gripped by a bloody civil war known as the Taiping Rebellion. Full-scale revolution had broken out. The rebel leaders were more open to Western ideas—including Western missionaries—than the Imperial government. It was a very exciting prospect but a frightening time.

The city was held by the rebels but was surrounded by Imperial government forces. The government was trying to starve the rebels out and turn the population against them. The city was shelled by artillery, and food and other supplies were blockaded. It created great hardship for the people.

Taylor immediately encountered problems in Shanghai. Foremost, he was all alone. There was no one to greet him at the pier, no friends, no place to stay and not a single person who even knew his name.

On top of everything else, the Chinese Evangelization Society had made no arrangements for a place for him to live. He was homeless and in quite a predicament.

"Mingled with thankfulness for deliverance from many dangers and joy at finding myself at last on Chinese soil came a vivid realization of the great distances between me and those I loved, and that I was a stranger in a strange land."

So he did the only thing he could: he went off in search of the London Missionary Society compound on the other side of the city. No one was expecting him, but he had a letter of introduction to these missionaries. He wound his way through the narrow, clogged streets of Shanghai and, with the help of God, found the mission.

The Chinese servants did not speak English, and Taylor understood none of their dialect. A confusing standoff followed, because Taylor had nowhere else to go. It was not until a young missionary named Dr. Edkins came along that Taylor was escorted into the compound. Seeing the situation, the leading missionary, Dr. Lockhart, invited Taylor to stay with him in a small apartment.

Barn! Barn! Barn!

The cannon fire exploded around the walls of the city. Gunfire was constant as a rebel attack from the city caught the government forces outside by surprise. Taylor watched and listened with the other missionaries. Many of the homes in the area had been destroyed from the fighting that had been going on so long. The heavy rain added mud and dread. When the fighting died down some, the missionaries walked through mud-filled streets to the North Gate after a crammed service at the London Mission chapel.

Soon the fighting escalated, and wounded and dead soldiers were brought back into the city. Taylor, drawing on his medical experience, examined one man. He had been shot through the arm and had a broken bone. Taylor began to bind the wound.

"Don't bother," Dr. Lockhart said.

"But why not? This can be cared for if the bleeding is stopped," Taylor replied.

"He must agree to go to the hospital. If he doesn't, he will just pull the dressings off."

Taylor did not understand but accepted what the doctor said. It was the beginning of many lessons about the very different Chinese culture. The next lesson was only minutes away. The rebels dragged five Imperial soldiers into the city. The men cried out when they saw the missionaries, hoping to find some mercy. Taylor was tempted to do something.

"There is nothing you can do," Dr. Lockhart said sadly.

"What will happen to them?"

"They will be beheaded within a few minutes," he said quietly, closing his eyes in prayer.

Hudson Taylor was seeing the cruel realities of war firsthand. His heart went out to the soldiers and to the suffering people trapped in the middle of the war.

During his first summer in Shanghai, Taylor suffered from severe headaches, probably from the heat that he was not used to back in England. He was studying the Mandarin Chinese dialect, the most common one, and searching for a place of his own. He finally found a small house in the native city and moved into it, living completely among the Chinese.

The misery he encountered among these

Chinese almost broke his heart. He was prepared for his own personal hardships but had never expected the daily assault of wretchedness and suffering that fell upon the average Chinese. He could walk in no direction—not even look out a little window—without witnessing a degree of anguish that brought him to tears. There was so little he could do about it.

Gradually, he developed his own evangelizing method in the area around his house. Knowing that sickness was so common, he dispensed what little medicine he could get and gave medical care to those who came. The number of sick visitors grew as word spread of the foreigner who lived among them. The chances to tell people about the Great Physician multiplied. Most listened politely and went their way. Many had heard the gospel because of the other missionaries living in Shanghai. A few were very interested and returned to learn more. Shortly, he was holding worship services for them.

The Chinese Evangelization Society had a reputation among missionaries for being undependable and too tight with money. Taylor did not know this when he left England, but he saw it in action in China. He frequently went many pay periods without receiving any money from the CES. When he eventually did, it was usually inadequate. In addition, there was almost no contact with the home committee. He learned to survive on a very scant amount of money and food, and to trust in God to meet his needs.

All these early lessons molded Taylor's thinking on how he should conduct himself before God and before man. The principles were being established for what would one day become the China Inland Mission.

During this time, Taylor remembered his calling from God. He was not to stay in a coastal city where missionaries were already working and spreading the word of salvation. He was to go inland, where hundreds of millions had never heard the name Jesus Christ.

Meanwhile, God was getting circumstances ready to send His servant into that dark, unreached interior.

5

Danger Inland

Hudson Taylor and Dr. Edkins slept soundly aboard the junk, a one-sail Chinese family houseboat. The only sound was the water lapping at the boat's sides and the gong of the night watchman. When the tide came in during the middle of the night, the anchor was pulled up, the sail hoisted, and the junk began silently sailing upriver.

But the two missionaries slept peacefully and did not awake until they were forty miles southwest of Shanghai, nearly to the city of Sungkiang.

Hudson Taylor was not one to let grass grow under his feet. Only eight months after landing in China, he was on his first evangelistic journey into the interior. The trip with Edkins was not sanctioned by British or Chinese authorities, which strictly controlled the movement of foreigners outside the treaty-port cities. Nonetheless, the chance to pass out tracts and talk to people in new areas presented itself, and Taylor jumped at it.

This first trip was not a big evangelistic success. No souls were known to be converted to Jesus. But a great deal was learned.

First, Taylor met a Buddhist recluse—what the people called a "holy man"—at the city temple. A group of yellow-robed Buddhist priests with shaved heads escorted the two missionaries deep inside the Sungkiang monastery, to a cell where the "holy man" had been walled up for many years. There were no doors or windows, just a small opening barely big enough for him to put his hand through, where food was passed in and the empty plate passed out. The devout priest had volunteered to be imprisoned like this as part of his religion. Taylor was virtually speechless, but he could pray.

"Hello, sir," Edkins said.

The man greeted them quietly from the dark cell.

"We are messengers of the Lord Jesus Christ," Edkins said.

"I don't know this god," the priest replied.

"He was sent from heaven, from the Father above, to save men's souls."

The priest was quiet for a moment. Edkins was about to go on, when the soft voice came back: "And how?"

Edkins then gave a brief but complete account of Mary and Joseph, Jesus' birth in a barn, His ministry, His death upon the cross and His resurrection.

"He rose from the dead? Then he was not dead," the priest said.

But Edkins assured him that Jesus had died a man's death and had risen again, pointing out that the act was the basis for victory over death through Jesus. The priest said nothing more. Seeing a quiet opportunity, Taylor and Edkins then prayed earnestly that the "glad tidings of great joy" that the priest had heard for the first time would become his salvation.

They never returned to that monastery, and there is no record of the priest's decision. Only God knows if his name is written in the scroll of life.

But Hudson Taylor saw the depth of China's pagan beliefs in that episode. The other priests accorded the imprisoned man great respect. The entire city revered the priests and the monastery.

While the Buddhist monks were open to the missionaries, the welcome was not as cordial from other parts of Sungkiang. Throughout the city, they were followed by an increasingly large and noisy rabble.

They decided it was time to leave and went back toward the river for their boat. But they went down the wrong street, and instead of ending up at the public ferry, they wound up at a private dock protected by fencing. The distracted missionaries had walked past gates without seeing them, and the uproarious crowd closed the gates, trapping the men against the water. The rowdy Chinese then swarmed onto the gates and the fences, taunting the men and watching to see what they would do next. Every time they called to a boat, the crowd laughed and jeered. None of the boatmen were going to stop for them.

It would have been an understandable moment to panic. They were in an unknown city, with no friends, no other Europeans—and probably no one in Shanghai knew they were there.

But the missionaries kept their wits. They prayed, then acted.

Taking a chance on a nearby passing boat, Taylor jumped from the dock into the boat. The boatmen made no objection and he pulled it to the side for Edkins to get in. Taylor wrote, "Off we went to the chagrin of our tormentors, who opened the gates and rushed to the waterside shouting tumultuously."

It was a narrow escape, and the episode made it clear that many people were not going to be warm to the gospel.

Before leaving the vicinity of Sungkiang,

however, they would learn one more lesson. While passing out the remainder of their tracts, they turned a bend in the road and came to the base of a nine-hundred-foot pagoda.

They met the priest in charge at the front door.

"We're visitors in your city. May we come inside?" Taylor asked in his improving Chinese.

The priest agreed and invited them in. The pagoda was quiet and still compared to the crowded, noisy streets of the city. The men ascended the pagoda stairs until they came to a gallery near the top, where they could look out on the city.

Taylor and Edkins stood beside each other, with the Buddhist priest near them. They were silent, and Taylor was in awe at the expanse of humanity that stretched in every direction. They could see for miles, and never did they come to the end of the roofs. There was the bustling city in the foreground, but beyond its ancient walls, the dense pace of tent-like roofs went on and on. The missionaries could see the spires of other pagodas in nearby cities, yet there was almost no break in the population. The cities seemed nearly to blend in to each other.

"So many souls," Taylor said in a hushed voice. Edkins remained silent.

"So many people who have never heard the name of Jesus . . . and only two of us here for a few weeks."

The immensity of the calling to inland China assumed a whole new meaning in Hudson Taylor's heart from that moment on.

Taylor went on another trip inland with the Rev. J.S. Burdon. This time he traveled up the Yangtze River to the large city of Tungchow. This city had a reputation as an evil place even among the Chinese: full of crime and hoodlums and drinking and unruly soldiers. The Chinese friends traveling with them tried to talk the men out of going, but Taylor and Burdon felt they had to speak the name of Jesus there, even if it was no more than handing out their tracts.

As they walked the seven miles to the city, their Chinese companions abandoned them out of fear. The mud in the road also became deeper, and a respectably dressed Chinese man stopped and urged them to turn back.

"You do not know what you are getting into. The city is filled with evil. The soldiers will drag you away," he told them pleadingly.

But their course was set.

"We cannot turn back," Taylor said. "No matter what happens, we cannot turn back."

The man was astonished. "But what is so important for you in Tungchow?" he asked. Taylor paused, then looked at the earnest man. "Lost souls."

"What?"

"We are followers of the Lord Jesus Christ, the only one who can save us," Taylor said, and he explained the gospel to the man.

"So you see, whether it means bonds, or imprisonment, or even death, we cannot leave Tungchow any longer without the gospel."

The man may not have "seen." But it was clear to Taylor and Burdon.

Yet the man's description and warning made them think. Were they headed for China's "Sodom and Gomorrah"?

Their fears were not far off. As their souls grew heavy on the outskirts of the city, they encouraged each other with Scripture and hymns. They approached the west gate of the city among a thickening throng of people who largely ignored the strangers.

But suddenly a tall, powerful, half-drunk man grabbed hold of Burdon. Before Taylor realized what was happening, several other ruffians grabbed him—and they began rushing the two into the city. The strong man left Burdon and took over Taylor, tormenting him as they went. He was knocked down over and over, then dragged by his collar until he was choking and bruised all over by the rough treatment.

In the midst of this torturous experience, Taylor remembered a verse his mother had quoted in her last letter:

> We speak of the realms of the blest,
> That country so bright and fair:
> And oft are its glories confessed—
> But what will it be, to be there!

Taylor had the very real impression that he was about to die. But God had other plans. The soldiers who had grabbed the missionaries were agruing about what they should do, with one loud faction insisting that the foreigners should be killed instantly. Eventually, the moderate group won out, and they were taken to the Mandarin, the city's leader.

Beaten, bloody and bruised, they stood before the Mandarin. He was from Shanghai and rebuked the soldiers for the shameful treatment. Taylor made the case for teaching the gospel in Tungchow, and the Mandarin listened quietly. He and his entourage also listened to Taylor explain the gospel and then had refreshments brought to them.

The Mandarin agreed to let them go into the city. Because of the brutal treatment they already had endured, Taylor asked for some guards, and the Mandarin agreed to that also. While the man was not a Christian, he seemed to be used mightily of God!

Taylor and Burdon distributed their booklets, did some short teaching when questions arose and were able to leave the city before nightfall. After dark they arrived safely back at the river with their Chinese friends, very thankful for God's protection.

Taylor was the only missionary consistently going inland from the treaty-port cities, so the Foreign Bible Society supplied him with all the Scriptures and tracts he needed. They also agreed to cover his expenses on these trips. On one major, early journey he traveled four hundred miles up the Yangtze River, preaching in fifty-eight cities and towns—most of which had never heard the gospel of Jesus.

These early travels inland had a huge impact on Taylor, clearly defining the immensity of his calling. It became ever more real in his heart. Also they taught him, more than ever, never to underestimate his need to rely totally on God.

6

Becoming Chinese to the Chinese

"Look at you!" exclaimed the British merchant in disgust.

Hudson Taylor smiled quietly at the large, well-dressed man confronting him, but did not reply. He was waiting in the port area of Shanghai to pick up some medicine, tracts and other supplies.

"You look like some kind of Chinese peasant," the man continued, then jabbed his finger in Taylor's direction.

Taylor continued to smile but found it difficult to remain silent.

"God called me to this country to tell the Chinese the good news about Jesus. The fashions I wear are for that end alone."

The proud British citizen would have none of it. To him, seeing a fellow British countryman wearing plain, backward Chinese clothing was an embarrassment: "It is a disgrace to the British Empire and to the Throne."

"I am not called to represent the British Empire or even Her Royal Majesty. I am a representative of God to the Chinese people."

"And you must represent the Almighty God in pajamas?"

Taylor paused. The man did not have Taylor's calling from God and probably would never understand. But it was important to Taylor that he always made his position clear, because he did not want to be a poor representative of Christ to his countrymen either.

"You sell tea, along with other merchants, right?"

The man nodded.

"Well, I'm sure you have the finest quality. But how do you display it? Is it wrapped in plain, brown sacks, or is it in pretty bundles with delicate pictures on the outside? And how do you dress when calling on customers? You make yourself as presentable as possible."

The merchant did not answer, knowing there was more.

"The point is, you make the tea and yourself inviting to the people. I too have the highest quality product. I am merely dressing in a way that makes the messenger of that product inviting. I am making them comfortable and maybe even confident in me. As Paul said, 'I have become all things to all, in hope that by all possible means I may save some.'"

The merchant pondered this for a few moments, then sucked his breath in deeply.

"I might dress the tea up. I certainly dress myself respectably. But I would never dress down the product or myself. Good day, sir."

And so it would go with many Europeans. Taylor's decision to dress as the Chinese, eat as the Chinese and live among the Chinese was not made lightly. He knew it would draw forth the scorn of others from his part of the world, and probably other missionaries as well. He already had worn Chinese clothing when on trips to the interior; but it was only for short times, and upon return he changed back immediately to his European clothes.

He felt the tug to more closely identify with the people. Paul was his model.

"And to the Jews I became as a Jew, that I might win Jews; to those who are under the law, as under the law, that I might win those who are under the law. . . .To the weak became I as weak, that I might win the weak. I have become all things to all men, that I might by all means save some."

Hudson Taylor took that Scripture verse and applied it to his life. To the Chinese, he became

Chinese, that he might win some to Christ. While his European comrades often disliked it, the decision would prove very fruitful for evangelizing.

Not long after this commitment was made, Taylor baptized into Christ his first Chinese convert, a man named Kuei-hua. Many more were to come.

Another reason for praise was sustenance from God. In October 1855 he received a second letter and large sum of money from W.T. Berger, a faithful Christian businessman in London who had a heart for the Chinese just as Taylor did. In his very encouraging letter, Berger told Taylor to expect great things from God—and the letter arrived just in time with regard to the money and the wisdom in it. Berger wrote:

> "Open thy mouth wide, and I will fill it." Oh, yes! God is not straitened. If we expect much from Him, He surely will not disappoint us.

God was building a relationship between the young missionary and this older Christian that would be vital to the future missionary work.

In the fall of 1855, Taylor found his first home in the interior of China, in a town named Sink'ai-ho. This city was on the island of Tsungming. One would not think of a coastal island being "inland," but it was outside the port city of Shanghai and full of Chinese who had not heard of Jesus. So it was an ideal place for Hudson Taylor. Kuei-hua and another convert, Ts'ien, went there with him, and they preached the gospel from this new position day and night.

He was able to rent a two-story house, providing adequate room to see patients and hold meetings. Soon Taylor settled into a routine of doing just that. He pushed himself at a hard pace, not knowing how long he might be allowed to remain there, outside the authority of the British and the Imperial Chinese governments.

The work progressed rapidly. Taylor had visions of establishing bands of believers who could be visited on a circuit such as the Methodists had created in the American West. He could feel the pressure of the assignment.

He wrote a letter asking for prayer:

> I sometimes feel a sense of responsibility that is quite oppressive—the only light-bearer among so many. But this is wrong. It is Jesus who is to shine in me. I am not left to my own resources. The two Christians are a great comfort.

While he was on a short trip back to Shanghai for supplies, his Christian helper Ts'ien raced back to get him. It seems the doctors and druggists in Sin-k'ai-ho did not like his charitable work. For a host of maladies that they could have cured, they extracted regular payments from patients to just relieve the symptoms. Now the foreigner, Taylor, was going around curing their patients and ruining their income! So they collected money among themselves and gave it to the Mandarin to have Taylor expelled from the island.

Taylor rushed back and discovered that an order had been given to round up some pirates first; then, later in the day, his two Chinese Christian helpers were to be taken before the Mandarin for questioning. They could receive three hundred to one thousand blows each if they gave the wrong answers.

"What should we do?" Kuei-hua asked.

"We will hold morning worship as always, asking the Lord for special protection; then we will go about our day," Taylor answered, with a little more confidence than he felt.

"But what about the Mandarin? Should we return to Shanghai?"

Taylor knew his friends were frightened. So was he. But they also knew they were free to leave anytime.

"I need to stay here with the work, and I trust in God."

And so the day proceeded with preaching and tending to patients as they came in. While he was finishing an operation on a woman's eye, the Mandarin and his men came down Taylor's street to his house. And they kept on going. They never stopped but continued on to the capital with their pirate prisoners.

God had delivered Taylor, Kuei-hua and Ts'ien.

7

God Provides a Mentor

Chang, a blacksmith on the island of Tsung-ming, and Sung, another resident of that island, were both converted to faith in Jesus by Taylor, and shortly thereafter they each openly declared themselves to be Christians. Chang closed his shop on Sundays, and the dramatic change in both their lives awakened interest among other Chinese in the area.

It was an exciting moment for Taylor as a small fire for the Lord began to spread. And with the threat from the Mandarin over, it looked as if the door was wide open for the gospel. That made it all the more difficult when the blow fell from a direction he was not expecting.

When Taylor returned to Shanghai on December 1, he found an official document waiting for him. The British Consul had been informed of his house on Tsung-ming and needed to talk to him about the matter. Taylor went to the Consul at once and truthfully explained the situation, requesting permission to stay where all now seemed peaceful. But the Consul reminded him that the treaty with the Chinese only allowed a foreigner to live in one of the five port cities. That ruled out Tsung-ming. If Taylor stayed in Tsung-ming, he could be made to pay a huge fine and forcibly removed.

The Consul's decision could be appealed, and Taylor planned to do just that.

It is not recorded how Taylor met William Burns, but God's hand was surely in it. Burns was famous among Christians for leading the Scottish revivals of 1839. He was a young evangelist in those days, but he went on to become a missionary to China. He shared a common calling with Taylor: tell the people of China about Jesus. And he brought to the relationship something Taylor needed—an older, wiser Christian to teach him, yet one who was still on fire for the Lord.

One of the first in-depth discussions they had while traveling together on their little boats was Taylor's conflict with the British authorities over his house and operation on Tsung-ming. Burns helped Taylor understand the spiritual points of his conflict.

Burns explained that it was not a question of forcing his legal rights or even being right.

"Those are secondary," he said as they slowly drifted toward the port of a river village. "It would be easy for God to simply make the circumstances right for you to live permanently on the island."

He paused. When Taylor said nothing, he continued.

"After all, Hudson, all authority has been given to Jesus. If the Lord has other plans for you, then what use is there fighting against them? And really, why would you want to?"

"No," Burns went on, "the servant of the Lord must not strive. He must be willing to be led by circumstances such as these. When the door is firmly closed, the Lord does not want you to go through it."

The spark of understanding suddenly dawned in Taylor, and he perked up. "Rely on the Divine will and trust God," he said with growing enthusiasm.

"Yes. Trust," Burns said with more excitement as the younger man caught hold of what he was saying. "Trust in God. Don't rely on man to accomplish man's desires. Trust in God alone."

Taylor did end up moving off the island, but he was able to go back and visit regularly and found that the Chinese Christians were continuing the work, although with less medicine.

It was a lesson that Taylor had already learned well, but Burns was the man who put it into perspective in this situation. The older man added one more thought.

"Nothing that our Lord permits can stop His work for long. If God wants you on Tsungming, He will lead you back there soon enough."

Taylor knew that was true, and he was greatly comforted by these words. He also realized he had been unduly discouraged.

The two men had one heart for the people of China, and it did not take long for them to develop a method of evangelization. Burns was a practical man of planning and, having more experience he had already formulated an effective approach. Taylor was only too happy to follow his advice.

First, they would choose an important city and stay there for about three weeks. They started on the outskirts, rising early every morning with a plan. Some days they went together, and some days they went separately. They would talk to any group of people that gathered, passing out tracts and gospels, and announcing the next meeting for that area. They often saw the same faces returning. Slowly, they moved into the crowded parts of the cities, and were able to walk down the crowded streets with all the busy vendors without causing a ruckus. They went to temples, schools, tea shops, and any other place that seemed appropriate.

Now it was time for Burns to learn a lesson from Taylor.

During the first few visits together, Burns noticed that the most serious listeners to the message went to Taylor to talk more. The riffraff always drifted toward Burns. The reason for this became clear: it was because Taylor wore Chinese dress while Burns wore foreign, European clothes.

Burns wrote about it to his elderly mother back in Scotland. "Four weeks ago I put on Chinese dress, which I am now wearing. Mr. Taylor had made this change a few months before, and I found that he was in consequence so much less hindered in preaching by the crowd that I concluded that it was my duty to follow his example."

Burns did not let pride get in the way of learning from a younger man. And he found such success with the change that he never returned to European clothes.

Swatow was the worst of cities, a Chinese vice center. The opium drug trade flourished there, as did all other manner of sin. And piracy was so bad that Chinese ships went there under a foreign flag so they could get British Navy protection.

While Taylor and Burns were back in Shang-hai, they met a Christian captain who had just returned from Swatow. The man's heart was heavy with the sinfulness of the city and the fact that no Christian minister was closer than one hundred and fifty miles from the city. Foreigners lived there, but they were mostly immoral and unbelievers.

While the man was speaking, Taylor felt called by God to go to Swatow. But he struggled against it because he had never before had a "spiritual father" such as Burns and did not want to separate from him. After a great deal of prayer and unrest, he chose to obey the call. But there was a surprise waiting for him when he unhappily told the news to Burns.

Taylor later wrote of the moment: "He listened with a strange look of surprise and pleasure rather than pain, and replied that he had determined that very night to tell me that he had heard the Lord's call to Swatow, and that his one regret had been the severance of our happy fellowship."

And so the Lord confirmed separately in their hearts what path He would lead them on.

On March 12, 1856, they arrived at the foreigner's settlement outside Swatow, about two miles from the city center. It would have been easy to set up housekeeping there, then travel into the city for their missionary work, but neither man gave that a moment's thought. Instead, they traveled into the crowded city. And their Chinese dress was a great help.

The city was located on a delta of the Han River, between two main channels. It was already bursting with people; the only way to expand the city was to fill the banks of the river, which was constantly being done. This made housing scarce for the two missionaries. Yet God brought together a series of apparent "coincidences," and they were able to find lodging in an attic. They could get to it only through a hole in its floor, but for both men it was perfect.

With the immoral trade that was everywhere in Swatow, it was no surprise that the missionaries' message of the gospel and righteous living was hated by many. Typically, the Chinese insult for missionaries was "foreign devil." But in Swatow they heard more "foreign dog" and "foreign pig"—both said with a hiss of hatred. The bitterness was deep and a completely new experience for both men.

They found warmer welcomes in the nearby towns surrounding Swatow. But still, the whole atmosphere was different from other parts of China. Most of the towns were walled. Often the little separate villages would be at war with neighboring villages. A horrendous tactic being used was to kidnap a leader from another village and demand ransom for his return. They would almost always torture their prisoner in the meantime. The entire countryside seemed more evil than usual. It required the men once again to completely trust God.

"There was nothing but the protection of God between us and the same treatment," Taylor wrote.

The southern heat also was a problem. In addition, Taylor had to learn the Cantonese dialect. So, as he studied, he kept a towel next to his books to wipe the continual sweat from his face. But the heat and even the dangers were tolerable; the sin and suffering were not.

"Sin does indeed reign here," Taylor wrote. "And, as always, those most to be pitied and whose case seems the most hopeless are the women. Looked upon as hardly having any soul, girls are sold here for wives or slaves."

A few nights before writing that letter, Taylor heard terrible screams coming from two women. They sounded as if they were in agony. He climbed down through the door in the floor and found one of his Chinese acquaintances outside.

"What is happening?" he asked.

The man looked out in the darkness as the screaming continued.

"I don't know for sure, but most likely they were newly bought women in a house nearby."

"Bought? You mean like slaves?"

"Yes, slaves," was the simple answer.

"But what is all the screaming about?" Taylor asked, getting more alarmed.

The man stopped staring into the darkness and looked at Taylor.

"They are being tortured into submission. Their new masters want to make sure they are obedient and will not try to run away." Then he looked back toward the darkness.

Taylor was speechless. Without looking at the missionary, his friend added one more thing: "That is very common here."

"Poor things. Poor things," Taylor said quietly.

The cries went on for about two hours.

It was in this atmosphere of immorality and accepted sin that Taylor and Burns toiled for the Lord. They talked, passed out tracts, held meetings and were encouraged by the response of many. They also held services in the foreigners' settlement and spread their work further out.

They wanted to open a hospital but were unable to until the chief Mandarin became sick and his people could not cure him. Taylor was sent for and was able to bring him back to health. The leader told them they could immediately set up a hospital for Swatow.

The ministry began to take hold in places, as a few Swatow-area Chinese accepted Christ and began attending worship services regularly. But just when they felt they were making progress, Taylor became sick. With the worst summer heat still ahead of them, Burns knew that the young missionary had to leave.

When free passage all the way back to Shanghai was offered, the men took it as the Lord's leading. If Taylor could round up enough medical equipment for the hospital, he would return with it and begin offering medical services.

So figuring they would see each other again in a few months, the good friends parted company.

But God had different paths charted for them. They never met again.

8

Rejection and Waiting on God

Hudson Taylor had not given much thought to marriage. He simply assumed that he would remain a bachelor all his life because of his calling to a vast foreign land. It made a great deal of earthly sense.

But he had not yet met Maria Dyer.

Maria was one of two orphan daughters of one of the London Missionary Society's earliest missionaries to China. She had lived in China until the age of ten, when her mother died. Her father had died much earlier. She was brought up by an uncle in London before hearing the call to China to be a helper to Miss Aldersley, an Englishwoman who ran a girls school in Ningpo, a port city south of Shanghai. She left England with the noble, but not faith-filled, idea of helping others. On the voyage to China, she entered into a new understanding of God, one in which she knew Jesus had done the work of cleansing her from sin. Her own actions, she realized, were insufficient. Romans 8:1 became alive to her:

"There is therefore now no condemnation to those who are in Christ Jesus."

Maria knew now that she really was a child of God. She entered upon her work with Miss Aldersley with a peace and joy that she had not known in England. She wasn't going just to do good, she was going to serve the Lord. From that voyage on, her heart was devoted to God. Her goal: teaching young ones and winning nonbelievers to the cause of Christ, that they might know the peace she had.

By the time Taylor's path crossed with Maria Dyer's, she had been working as an assistant to Miss Aldersley for some time. A series of events had made it impossible for him to get the needed medical supplies and return to Swatow and Burns. He ended up visiting Ningpo to help a friend at the missionary hospital there.

Maria immediately recognized a kindred spirit for the Lord in Hudson Taylor. But they saw each other only occasionally. They met each other at friends' homes, and he was attracted to her because of her forthright way and tender heart. As they talked, he found her to be a like-minded person on fire for Jesus—and she began to fill a place in his heart.

"That was what drew out my interest," Hudson would write many years later. "She was spiritually minded, as her work proved. Even then she was a true missionary."

As his feelings intensified, Hudson consciously tried to banish Maria from his thoughts.

After all, he thought, *I cannot have a wife and family along with the demands that are on my life from God. And I must admit that I also have no earthly means to support a family.*

Thus he fought against the growing desires in his heart.

Meanwhile, a bubbling dispute between the British and the Chinese was boiling over into a full-scale war. The "Opium War" had ended fourteen years earlier with a British victory that resulted in more trade and, particularly, the treaty ports for foreigners. But since that time, the British had continued pushing the Chinese Emperor to legalize imported opium. The Emperor refused to sanction the powerful drug, which he called the "flowing poison."

Even though a large part of the British Parliament was opposed to the action, powerful elements in the government and the army saw the opportunity for vast profits, and soon British naval guns were pounding the southern Chinese port city of Canton. That battle rippled throughout China to Ningpo, which housed a large Cantonese population.

A plan was hatched to kill all of the foreigners in Ningpo. The plot was found out just in time, but the threat was now very real. Several missionaries decided to send their wives to the safer city of Shanghai. The responsibility to accompany the group fell to Hudson Taylor. There was no one more suitable. He was free to make the trip, and he knew the Shanghai dialect and the city well.

But it meant leaving Ningpo, and Maria.

After just seven weeks in Ningpo, Hudson was gone. And to Maria's surprise, she found she missed him deeply. She confided to the Lord her love for him. But she did not tell anyone on earth.

He is not always well understood by those in the foreign community, she thought to herself. *His wearing of Chinese clothing and identifying so closely with the Chinese is frequently not appreciated. But there is so much more to him than what shows on the surface.*

Maria Dyer saw in Hudson Taylor's actions a man after God's heart.

The trip was uneventful, but Taylor was required to stay with the families because the fathers were remaining in Ningpo. So he set up his evangelizing again and watched out for the needs of the missionary families under his care.

He also chose this moment to cut his ties with the Chinese Evangelization Society. He did this because he was utterly convinced that debt was unacceptable, not biblical, and that he should not be a part of it. For three years he had labored to stay out of debt. But the majority of the CES board was comfortable with debt, and in fact had a large one. In Christian love, without animosity or judgment, he resigned from the organization. To the credit of Taylor and the members of the CES, the parting was completely in friendship, and he remained in fellowship with many CES members for decades to come.

But now his heart was in a state of turmoil. He longed to see and talk to Maria again. But that did not seem to be a possibility. He cast this growing care upon the Lord but could get no peace. He knew in his heart that Maria was the woman for him, the one whom God had placed in his life. So in early 1857 he carefully crafted a letter to her and asked her to marry him. He mailed the letter, then left the issue in God's hands as patiently as he could. He had no idea whether Maria even returned his affections.

He waited for the reply—and waited and waited. Weeks passed, and he fought feelings of anxiety.

Finally, the letter arrived. In her pretty feminine handwriting, she quite bluntly told him that what he desired was impossible and to please not bring up the subject again. Despite his prayer, it was like a blow to the stomach.

His heart was broken over the letter. The rejection was so harsh and permanent, it did not even sound like Maria's gentle spirit.

And, indeed, it was not. Miss Aldersley had all but dictated the letter over Maria's tears. Miss Aldersley was painfully frank about it.

"Mr. Taylor! That young, poor, unconnected nobody! How dare he presume to think of such a thing? Of course the proposal must be refused at once, and that finally!" she told Maria.

Hudson Taylor dressed like a Chinese peasant, lived in shacks among the Chinese and had no visible means to support himself, let alone a wife and even children, Miss Aldersley argued. And in addition, he was from a lower social level, which was an important consideration for many in English society.

There was nothing that Maria could say to change Miss Aldersley's mind. It was unthinkable to Miss Aldersley to let the girl in her charge marry a man with seemingly so little to offer. Besides, the friends Maria was staying with at the time strongly reinforced Miss Aldersley's decision. So she required Maria to write the rejection letter in no uncertain terms.

Hudson Taylor had no idea that she felt just the opposite from her letter. So he fell back into the arms he knew were strong enough to hold him up in his sorrow.

As summer came, the warring between England and China subsided and the possibility for aggressive evangelism in Ningpo arose. Several families returned, and Taylor was free to go to the city where Maria was. But he was not free in spirit to see her or even speak to her. They were not to try to contact each other in any way. Both of them submitted to Miss Aldersley's requirement.

Taylor still did not know at this point that Maria returned his deep feelings for her. However, because of the nature of people, word got around the Ningpo foreign community that Taylor had proposed and that Maria had rejected him only at the insistence of Miss Aldersley. That rumor could not help but make its way back to Hudson's ears, and he yearned to know the truth. An afternoon deluge of rain required Maria Dyer to stay behind after a society meeting on a very fortunate day. Hudson happened to be with the husband of the woman in whose parlor Maria was staying to wait out the downpour.

Suddenly there was an opportunity for some friends of both young people to take the situation into their own hands. The man invited Hudson inside to visit with his wife and Maria Dyer.

When he walked into the room, he saw the woman he loved far above any other person on earth. Though other ladies were in the room, he barely noticed them. He sat next to Maria on the couch, and forty years later he would recall the moment.

"We sat side by side on the sofa, her hand clasped in mine. It never cooled—my love for her. It has not cooled now."

He had intended only to ask her guardian for permission to write her. But within moments he did what he never thought possible: out spilled his feelings for her in front of everyone, still without his knowing for sure if she felt the same way. And further, he again asked her to marry him, right there!

There were smiles and murmurings among those in the room, and not a little embarrassment.

But within minutes Maria had also let her emotions come rushing out, and she agreed to marry him. The sacred moment was witnessed by everyone present, and complete silence fell over the group. Knowing the situation with Miss Aldersley, it was hard to know what to say. Finally, Taylor did the thing he knew best to do.

"Let's take it all to the Lord in prayer," he said.

With Maria's promise out, and pressure from new friends to allow the wedding, there was nothing Miss Aldersley could do but agree to the marriage. They were married on January 20, 1858, Maria in a gray silk wedding gown and Hudson in his Chinese dress. It was a simple ceremony, but many people in attendance remembered it even years later because it was between two people becoming one, in devotion to God.

The marriage was a joy to Hudson and Maria from the first day.

"Oh, to be married to the one you do love, and love tenderly and devotedly—that is bliss beyond the power of words to express or imagination to conceive," he wrote.

9

Faithful Commitments

God was all-sufficient in the Taylors' weakness. Just the two of them launched out on faith in ministry in Ningpo, but both had faith equal to the task ahead.

"I was left an orphan in a far-off land," Maria said. "God has been my Father all these years; and do you think I shall be afraid to trust Him now?"

Their faith in the Father was well-placed. God brought into their lives souls hungry for the gospel. Also, very important at this time, He brought men and women that, once converted, became soul-winners themselves.

An early convert was Fang Neng-Kuei, a basket maker, who was introduced to the Taylors by Nyi, whom Taylor had led to Christ earlier. Neng-Kuei grasped the message of Christ completely and began bringing his basket-making friends to the meetings. Taylor wanted to teach these men the deep things of living in Christ. At this point in his ministry, he strove for mature, faithful Christians who could take an intimate knowledge of God to their people. These folks soon had to meet testing of the depth of their faith.

When word got around that the basket makers were becoming Christians, a fair amount of persecution began. They were teased, their businesses suffered, their families shunned them, and sometimes they were physically threatened. This testing of their faith was hard, and Taylor was saddened to see that one after another of the basket makers stopped attending the worship meetings. Finally, only Fang was left.

Would Fang drop out also? No. His faith was firmly grounded in the Rock, and he remained strong and true. His commitment to Christ proved deep. Also the persecution had the effect of sharpening his defense of the gospel, creating an effective evangelist to his own people.

One day Fang was explaining to some women in an upper-class Chinese home that he could not make the baskets they wanted for idol worship because he was a follower of the one and only true God.

"What!" one of the women said. "Not make baskets for holding incense? Refuse an order for anything to be used in the service of the gods?"

"Do not be angry, ladies," Fang replied. "I am sorry not to comply with your wishes, but I cannot make or sell anything for the worship of idols."

"And why not?" came the astonished, indignant question.

"I am a believer in the Lord Jesus," he said respectfully, but firmly, "a worshiper of the true and living God." He then explained the gospel to them. But they were wholly unready to hear it. They made such a mocking commotion that they caught the attention of Wang Lae-djun, a painter working on their house.

Wang had been searching for truth for many years, trying one religion after another. When the women tired of the subject and tottered off, annoyed, he found Fang.

"What was that you were saying. Wang asked. Fang explained his reason for not making baskets for idol worship.

"I can serve only one master; that is the Lord Jesus Christ," he said.

"And you claim He rose from the grave, after being dead for three days?"

"Yes. That is the special hope that all followers of Jesus have. Because He conquered death, and has all power over it, we do not fear death.

When we die in this earthly body, and that earthly body," he said, poking at Wang's paint-stained Chinese pajamas, "we get a new body in heaven that will last forever."

This was something Wang had never heard before in the other religions—a guarantee regarding the afterlife. Not long after this meeting, Wang accepted Christ as his Savior. That was a huge step for the kingdom of God on earth, because Wang went on to become a powerful evangelist for his people and pastor of a large, vibrant church. He remained a close friend of Hudson Taylor for many years.

His conversion and earthly works can be traced to Fang's faithfulness in turning down the idol money because it did not honor Jesus. And Fang's steadfast faith was born of the trials he had endured early as a believer.

On Febuary 9, less than three weeks after their wedding, Maria took ill. She had internal inflammation and was fading quickly. Her temples were hollow, her eyes sunken, her features shriveling. As Hudson knelt beside her in prayer, united with a cluster of Christians from all over Ningpo praying for her, he thought he was watching his bride die.

Suddenly it occurred to him to try Dr. Parker, a missionary-doctor friend who had set up a hospital in Ningpo, two miles away. Hudson was not sure if Maria would last that long without him, but he took off quickly for the doctor.

While running the distance, the promise came to his mind, "Call upon Me in the day of trouble; I will deliver you, and you shall glorify Me." Taylor had sudden peace in his pounding heart. He found Dr. Parker and the men raced back, although Taylor was not fearful now. When they arrived, they saw in an instant a miracle: Maria's countenance was one of returning health. In just that hour or so, the Great Physician had done His work. The death that seemed so near was cast far away. There was no purpose for Dr. Parker even to be there. Maria recovered quickly, and both Taylors were further strengthened in their trust in God.

In September 1859 Dr. Parker's wife died, leaving him with several small children. In such a circumstance he was unable to continue operating the Ningpo hospital and was forced to return to England. He approached Taylor about taking over the operation. That was not in the young missionary's plans, but he knew enough to seek the Lord rather than follow his own plan.

After much prayer he and Maria agreed to take on the hospital, "relying solely on the faithfulness of a prayer-hearing God to furnish means for its support." Dr. Parker had used his income as a practicing physician to support the work of the hospital. That income now ceased.

So the commitment to no debt would be a test for the Taylors and a testimony for the Chinese—because as soon as it became known that the hospital would not borrow money, and knowing that no one had any income like that of Dr. Parker, the Chinese watched eagerly to see what the foreigners' God would do.

They did not have to wait long. First, He put in the hearts of the group of worshiping Christians—known as the Bridge Street group—the desire to serve the Lord by volunteering at the hospital. That reduced expenses. But it did much more.

Dr. Parker had hired Chinese to help him in the work. But these new men and women were doing it to serve God and their fellow men and women. The joy of Jesus Christ permeated the hospital. The patients, up to fifty at times, could not explain the new atmosphere, but they enjoyed it. They even accepted the continual telling of the gospel because it came with such freshness and love.

However, the testing of faith was coming. The money Dr. Parker left behind for the hospital was being spent, and the supplies were running out. One morning, the cook told Hudson that the last bag of rice was opened and disappearing. There could be no flippancy now about trusting God: fifty sick people were relying on the Taylors.

But Hudson Taylor was relying on a much higher authority. He replied simply to the matter of the disappearing food: "Then the Lord's time for helping us must be close at hand."

Indeed it was. For in the mail was a check to Taylor from William T. Berger for fifty English pounds, enough to buy plenty of food and supplies. Mr. Berger, who lived in London, had the same zeal as Taylor for evangelizing China, but God used him differently. A successful business -man, Berger had begun sending Taylor money a few years earlier. At that time he had written to Taylor, "Open thy mouth wide, and I will fill it.' Oh, yes! God is not straitened. If we expect much from Him, He surely will not disappoint us."

That proved true. God was not disappointing the Taylors and their circle of believers. He was filling the faithful in Ningpo for everyone to see. Hudson's reliance on God to provide for his needs was an opportunity for God to show His power.

The relationship with Berger would prove to be a very fruitful one for Taylor's calling: the future evangelizing of inland China.

10

The Sands of Brighton

The Taylors' first daughter, Grace, was born later in 1859. The little family and their friends were filled with joy at the new arrival. But Hudson Taylor came down with tuberculosis within a year. It was a serious disease, and his health declined until he decided it would be better for the family to return to England.

So after seven years of work in China, he sailed back to England. Although he still had no money, he was a richer man going home, because he now had a dear wife, a child, new friends and many Chinese Christians in the kingdom because of the work of the Holy Spirit through him. But he also went back a very sick man, with a long road of recovery ahead of him.

The five years that the Taylors spent in England are known as the "hidden years," because much of the time is lost to the mists of history.

Neither of the Taylors kept a continuous diary at this time.

Hudson spent much of his time resting, corresponding and translating the New Testament and some hymns into the Ningpo dialect of Chinese. Also, two children were born to the Taylors during this time.

Near the end of his time in England, Hudson began wrestling anew with the demands of China. But this time, the burden for the Chinese took him down a different road. He knew he needed tremendous help to reach the literally hundreds of millions of Chinese—a million of whom were dying every month without the comfort of Christ. He felt he should begin to pray, in faith, expecting an answer, for helpers in the field. He was reading out of Ezekiel, whom God called to be a watchman for Israel. "If the watchman warns the people and they do not repent, the wicked will surely be condemned," he read. But God further declared: "If you neglect to warn them, so that they do not know to repent, they will still be condemned, but their blood will I require at your hand."

He struggled mightily with this. It was his call to tell the Chinese of Christ.

"I knew God was speaking. I knew also that, in answer to prayer, evangelists would be given and their support secured—because the name of Jesus is worthy. But at that point, unbelief rushed in." He worried that if he were to gather a band of men to go to inland China, they still might all starve or be killed in some way. That is what he labeled his "unbelief."

On June 25, 1865, Taylor, tired and ill, went to the seaside town of Brighton with some friends. His health started improving, but he could not even attend worship with them because he was so distraught over what God wanted of him. He was in constant communion with the Lord. Then, on the sands of Brighton, a new and wonderful understanding came to him.

"Why, if we are obeying the Lord, the responsibility rests with Him, not with us!" Taylor wrote. "You, Lord," he cried with relief that was unutterable, "You shall have all the burden! At Your bidding, as Your servant I go forward, leaving results with You."

It was an epiphany for Taylor. Not only could he rely on God for all his personal needs, he could rely on Him to provide for the needs of his ministry, too. Taylor did not need to carry anything that was "of the Lord," for God would bear the load for him. He wrote the following in his Bible: "Prayed for twenty-four willing, skillful laborers at Brighton, June 25, 1865."

For the first time, he prayed for a specific number of workers, expecting God to answer the prayer. He now understood that it was the Lord's responsibility.

Hudson Taylor finally had peace.

And he had the beginnings of the China Inland Mission.

By late 1865 he had regained his full health, and Maria thought that Brighton's brisk air had done wonders for her husband—yet it was much more than physical healing that renewed Hudson Taylor.

Two key players in the future of the China Inland Mission were developed at this time. One was George Müller, who was doing a mighty work of faith among orphans in England, and who shared Taylor's views on allowing God to provide all. Müller had decided many years earlier that he would not ask man for anything but that he would take all his requests directly to God. He did it quite simply to prove that God was faithful and would keep His promise to meet all our needs. Müller's life was a testimony to God's faithfulness. He was a great encouragement for Taylor and was very generous with the blessings of God. The other was William Berger, mentioned earlier, who was willing to devote vast amounts of his wealth to the cause as God directed. Berger became the leader of the China Inland Mission at the home end, an indispensable arm in England for Taylor.

One other important series of events happened during this period in England. Taylor was asked to write an appeal for China in the *Baptist Magazine*. However, after reading it, the editor was so touched that he urged him to publish it as a pamphlet for wide distribution. Taylor did so, publishing what became known as *China's Spiritual Needs and Claims*.

Taylor, who did not yet have a reputation as a speaker and who was only starting to be known from his pamphlet, persuaded the leaders of a large Christian conference to let him say a few words about China.

When his turn came, he was nervous. He stood at the podium and looked at the intelligent, influential people—people who cared deeply about spiritual matters—and told the personal story of "the callous fishermen."

Nearing the city of Sungkiang, Hudson and a Chinese friend, Peter, had been on a boat, preparing to go ashore together . . . when he was startled by a sudden splash and heard a cry that told of a man overboard. Springing at once on deck, he looked around and missed Peter.

"Yes," exclaimed the boatman. "It was over there—he is sure to drown!"

To drop the sail and jump into the water was not feasible because the tide was running out, and the low, shrubless shore did not provide a landmark. Searching everywhere in agony, Taylor caught sight of some fishermen with a dragnet—just the thing he needed.

"Come," he cried as his hope revived, "drag over this spot. A man is drowning!"

"It is not convenient," was the amazing reply.

"Don't talk of convenience! Quickly, come—or it will be too late!"

"We are busy fishing."

"Never mind your fishing! Come—only come at once! I will pay you well."

"How much will you give us?"

"Five dollars! Only don't stand talking. Save the man's life without delay."

"Too little!" they shouted across the water. "We will not come for less than thirty dollars."

"I don't have that much with me! But I will give you all I've got."

And how much might that be?"

"Oh, I don't know. About fourteen dollars."

Upon this they came, and the first time they passed the net through the water they brought up the missing man. But all Taylor's efforts to restore his breathing were in vain. It was only too plain that life was gone, sacrificed to the heartless indifference of those who might easily have saved it.

As he finished the tale, a burning sense of indignation swept over the great audience. The crowd was outraged at the lack of concern of the fishermen.

But as his earnest voice went on, conviction struck home just as deeply to the large gathering: they realized there was an allegory for them in the story.

"Is the body, then, of so much more value than the soul? We condemn those heathen fishermen. We say they were guilty of the man's death because they could easily have saved him and did not do it," Taylor said, intensifying his speech.

Then he hammered home the point:

"But what of the millions whom we leave to perish, and that eternally? What of the plain command: 'Go into all the world and preach the gospel to every creature'? Can we ignore the searching question inspired by God Himself: 'If you deliver not those who are drawn toward death, and those who are ready to be slain; if you say, "Surely we did not know this" —does not He who weighs the hearts consider it? He who keeps your soul, does He not know it? And will He not render to each man according to his deeds?'"

Taylor was developing into a prophet, one who would teach much of the Christian world about the tremendous spiritual needs of China.

11

Criticism and Rebellion

Hudson Taylor's prayer for twenty four workers was answered within a year.

On May 26, 1866, the Taylors left London to return to China. With them were twenty two missionaries, with several more coming on the next ship. Most of the people were working-class Christians. Most of them had little formal training, but they had great faith. It was a complete answer to his specific prayer on the sandy beaches of Brighton.

On the way to China, the energetic group of mostly young missionaries converted almost the entire crew of the ship.

Not everything would go as smoothly on land.

Taylor was committed to the way of evangelizing the Chinese that he had developed with William Burns. He felt sure it was of God, and when he was convinced of that, he was not likely to change. The China Inland Mission, as it was now being referred to officially, would be operated without debt and by asking only the heavenly Father for needs. There would be no direct appeals for donations—a very unusual step but a step that George Müller's faith-filled actions were already proving in his orphanage ministry.

In addition, all missionaries would dress as the Chinese dress and live among the Chinese, not in any foreign settlements. Taylor introduced one other controversial innovation: he allowed single women to be missionaries to the Chinese.

These techniques drew a lot of criticism, even from other missionaries. While some resistance may have had to do with pride—such as not wanting to wear Chinese clothes—not all of it was senseless or narrow-minded. There were some solid reasons for not allowing single women in a mission field such as China. The most obvious was safety: the Chinese were often very cruel to their own women—such as buying and selling them as slaves and wives. They also could be very hostile to foreigners. The threat to any missionary was great, but when everything was added up, the threat to single women was even more substantial.

Hudson Taylor was well aware of these dangers. But he also had seen how effective women were in reaching Chinese women. Because of the cultural differences, they could speak to them openly of the gospel in ways men could not.

Seven of the first group of twenty four were single women.

Taylor took all of the precautions he knew to take. The single women were paired off as co-workers and usually ministered with a missionary family. They were never sent out alone. But after doing what he thought best, he entrusted them to the Lord, just as he entrusted himself and his family.

Most of the missionaries settled into stations expanding toward the interior from the port cities, particularly out of the Shanghai area. He set up a temporary base in the large city of Hangchow, which was located between Shanghai and Ningpo, and tried to fit each one to his abilities.

A good example was Mr. Rudland, who had worked in a forge in Cambridgeshire, England before hearing the call to China. His employer had tried to get him not to go by showing him a book in Chinese characters.

"This is the way they write their language. Do you think you could ever learn that?"

"Has anybody else learned it?" Rudland asked.

"Maybe a few."

"Then why not I?" he asked.

Rudland's faith was simple but deep. He was a very hard and diligent worker. But once in China, try as he might, he could not learn to read the language. It looked just like a hopeless tangle of lines. Soon he was getting headaches. Undoubtedly his employer's words came back to mind.

But Taylor found a solution.

"Could you help me?" he asked Rudland one day during the young man's studies.

"I would be glad to. But what can I do?"

"I'm having a problem with the printing press," Taylor said, explaining that as long as there was direct supervision, the Chinese workers did well. But as soon as they were left on their own, the work nearly came to a stop.

"I don't have time to watch over them. Do you think you could manage things for me?"

"I would very much like to. But I don't know anything about printing."

"Just go in and start at the beginning. The workers will show you how everything works. And your just being there will encourage them to keep at the job."

"I'll give it a try," Rudland said.

He was a man who worked best with his hands, and a man who quickly picked up the spoken language. Taylor had placed him in an environment where he was more comfortable than when studying books. And once he could speak Chinese well, he became an effective worker for the China Inland Mission.

Rudland ultimately opened thirty-seven missionary stations. In connection with those and his own center, more than three thousand Chinese were baptized into Christ. Rudland also translated the New Testament and part of the Old Testament into the Chinese dialect of his mission center!

Stories like Rudland's were almost commonplace in the Chinese Inland Mission, as God worked His way on a daily basis. But there were others that were much sadder.

Within about six months after arriving in China with the first group of twenty-four missionaries, one group, stationed down the road from Hang-chow in a city named Siaoshan, rebelled. They chose to stop wearing Chinese clothing. The reasons were not all clear, but this particular group chose to go against most of Taylor's rules for the mission. It was a costly decision for everyone.

Shortly after they returned to wearing their European clothes, the ruling Mandarin expelled them from the city. As long as they were low-key and did not cause a ruckus, he had allowed them to stay. But with the change to foreign clothes, they attracted all the wrong attention.

On the night of January 28, the Mandarin

came upon them with his soldiers and ordered them to leave the city immediately. To impress his authority on them, he took the Chinese evangelist, Tsiu, and had him severely beaten. Taylor had let Tsiu go with them at a great sacrifice to his own operation. Now Tsiu was forced to return, along with the missionaries.

With that, whatever ministry they had begun to build in Siaoshan was finished.

The group returned to Hangchow. Taylor did not judge them. He tried to draw the dejected missionaries into the bustle of hospital duties going on. But they became like a poison in the camp. Their rebellious attitude created division within the missionary group there. It also encouraged opposition to the China Inland Mission among some other missionaries—and one in particular, who, although a stranger, wrote terrible accusations about Taylor back to Saint Hill in London, where Berger had set up the home operations. This man had worked in China many years and was respected. But he did not even know Taylor. Also, some of the embittered missionaries began writing letters with untruthful accusations to Saint Hill. All these letters were a shock when they arrived in the hands of William Berger. Taylor was completely unaware of them at first, because none of the missionaries had come to him with the complaints.

But Berger was a true friend, and he knew Taylor's heart. The letters, while stunning, did not seem likely to be accurate. He sent Taylor copies of the main critical letter from the elder missionary, and then wrote supportively.

> My earnest prayer to cod is that you may not be further moved by the letter than the Lord would have you be; and may He give the right spirit and the wisdom that will enable us both to do that which will please Him.
>
> The difficulties at home are neither few nor slight, but yours are truly mountainous. You need every sympathy and prayer; and to be sure, my dear Brother, whatever Mr. ______ may have penned, you hold the same place in our hearts as before. That God will supply you and me with increasing wisdom and ability for the work to which He has called us, we need neither fear nor doubt.

Taylor chose not to answer the accusations in any way. He feared that any answers would begin a larger, visible argument. If the Chinese were to see the Christians fighting among themselves—regardless of whether there was any justification—the cause of Christ could be marred. The witness he had worked so hard to develop could be lost. He would not take that chance. Instead, he entrusted the entire attack to the Lord. God had called him to China. He had now provided co-workers—and He had a plan. Taylor was sure that his Lord would carry him through these troubles as He had through so many others.

Meanwhile, Berger continued to be a faithful friend and co-worker. God clearly had chosen the right man to anchor Taylor's operations at home. While this unpleasant situation continued much longer than either man would have thought, Berger continued to write letters of encouragement to Taylor.

In one of these letters, written on May 19, 1867, Berger urged Taylor to take a more strategic view of the operation. In a sense the older man seemed to have a better grasp at that moment of the great potential of the mission.

> It seems to me we must enlarge our field of vision in regard to this work; that you must not undertake so much of the detail, but a more enlarged oversight; that you must not have so many immediately depending on you. Oh, what need for wisdom in every step of this work!

God would enlarge the field greatly, but first He would allow Taylor to be tested. The testing of his faith would develop the perseverance needed for the task ahead.

12

Supreme Sacrifice

The first summer back in China was intensely hot, even for China. The temperature often read 103 degrees indoors, and sickness and disease were rampant in the cities. Maria was very ill, and all of the children suffered from some sort of sickness. But Grace, now 8, was the most ill. In her weakened state she contracted hydrocephalus.

The condition meant certain death for the girl, and Hudson and Maria Taylor knew that nothing short of a miracle from God would save their daughter. Taylor wrote to Berger about the situation, admitting that he knew exactly of this danger when he put his family on the altar of spreading God's kingdom in China. He had never doubted the reality of this threat. Yet when it became real, it came heavily upon him.

"I am trying to pen a few lines by the couch on which my darling little Gracie lies dying," he wrote Berger. "Dear brother, our flesh and our heart fail, but God is the strength of our heart and our portion forever. . . . He has not left us now."

But Gracie died soon after that. Her death almost broke her parents' hearts. But they held firmly to the truth, and they knew in their spirits that she was with the Lord.

To his mother, an aching Hudson Taylor wrote: "Our dear little Gracie, how we miss her! As I take walks I used to take with her tripping at my side, the thoughts come anew like a throb of agony. Is it possible that I will never more feel the pressure of that little hand, never more hear the sweet prattle of those dear lips, never more see the sparkle of those bright eyes? And yet she is not lost."

Showing the true measure of his faith, he continued, "I would not have her back again. She is far holier, far happier, than she could ever have been here."

The loss of Gracie was just one more lesson in trusting God—the hardest yet.

The Taylors remained faithful to their calling. The work continued. After sixteen months back in China, there were fifty Chinese worshiping regularly under Wang, the man to whom Fang had been a Christian example. And there were many more converts in other cities where China Inland Mission missionaries were doing God's work.

As the work grew and flourished, the dangers and sickness in the Taylor family continued to mount. In 1869, about two years after Gracie died, their little son Samuel fell suddenly into a coma and quickly died. Two children had now been sacrificed for China. The rest struggled with ill health.

Hudson, giving thanks always in all things—as the Bible teaches—again wrote to his friend Berger:

> I have seen them awake for the last time in China. Two of our little ones we have no anxiety about; they rest in Jesus' bosom. And now, dear Brother, though the tears will not be stayed, I do thank God for permitting one so unworthy to take any part in this great work, and do not regret having engaged and being engaged in it. It is His work, not mine nor yours; and yet it is ours—not because we are engaged in it, but because we are His, and one with Him whose work it is.

Hudson Taylor was willing to sacrifice anything for his calling from God. He was moving to the point of totally trusting God for everything. But he was not a rash, unwise man. He was also willing to do what seemed right to spare his children. So finally, in 1869, he and Maria made the painful decision to send all of the children except their youngest child back to the healthier climate of England.

But the stoniest ground in his life, the greatest testing, had yet to arrive.

On July 7 Maria gave birth to their seventh child, their fifth son. Their joy was brief. In the heat and disease of the country, the child died only a week later from the dreaded cholera.

The birth, the heat and the infant's death marked the beginning of the end for Maria's earthly body. But as with the deaths of the three children, the heartache was mixed with the joy that only a follower of Jesus can know. Here is a portion of a telling conversation Hudson recorded when the morning light brought to view the gray death hue on his beloved Maria's face:

"My darling, do you know that you are dying?"

"Can it be so? I feel no pain, only weariness."

"Yes, you are going Home. You will soon be with Jesus."

"I am so sorry," she said.

"You are not sorry to go to be with Jesus, are you?"

Hudson never forgot the look with which she answered, "Oh no! It is not that . . . I cannot be sorry to go to Him; but it does grieve me to leave you alone at such a time. Yet He will be with you and meet all your needs."

Not much later, Maria died, on July 23, 1870, after only twelve years of marriage to Hudson Taylor. While short, the years were filled with love, joy and a faithful walk together.

He mourned the loss of Maria deeply and again relied on God to carry him through his grief. "With the weakness of a child I have the rest of a child. I know my Father reigns."

Hudson Taylor had now buried three dear children and his cherished wife in the soil of China—all for the cause of taking the gospel of Jesus Christ to the Chinese. And still the blows kept falling on him. He must have felt some fellowship with Job at this point, for now his own health began to falter so seriously that friends thought he might be following his wife Home.

"How lonesome were the weary hours when confined to my room. How I missed my wife and the little pattering footsteps of the children far away in England!" But Taylor remembered God's promise: "Whosoever shall drink of the water that I shall give him shall never thirst." He believed God's promises to be as real as the bed he lay on. While aching for his wife and children, he called out to God.

"Lord, You promised! You promised me that I should never thirst."

And God filled him every time—so regularly that he wondered out loud if Maria could be enjoying any more of the presence of Christ than he was, alone in his bedroom.

Yet his health continued to decline. Friends urged him to return to England for a short recuperation, and he agreed. He ended up spending two years in his home country. While there, he created the Council of Christian Friends. Berger was now an elderly man and simply too old to carry on the rapidly expanding duties of the China Inland Mission. This Council would help do Taylor's work at home, and that of Berger.

Near the end of these two years in England, Taylor remarried. He and Maria had known Jennie Faulding for many years. She was a longtime missionary to China, and they had all labored together for the gospel. In Jennie, Taylor knew a woman who loved the Lord, loved his children and was devoted to the work in China. The newly married couple returned to China in October 1872.

He spent some time strengthening the growing mission, which now had thirty members in thirteen mission stations. Then he began to enlarge his borders.

In 1874 he set out for Hankow to search out the furthest parts of inland China. From there he could envision the rest of the huge Chinese nation, which stretched from the southern tropics on the Burma border to the mountains of Tibet and the cold plains of Mongolia. In all that vastness there was scarcely a messenger of Christ. More than one hundred and eighty million people living in darkness.

One more setback remained. While in Hankow, he fell and injured his back. That, combined with his poor health, forced him to return to England once again.

Back home, he hit the lowest point of his life. The fall began a slow paralysis, starting in his legs and moving up. At the worst point he was bedridden and could not even move his arms to write. Circumstance had required that his four surviving children, who were being cared for by a devoted family friend who took very ill, be dispersed among relatives.

He was indeed at the lowest point in his life.

Hudson Taylor had lost three children and his dear first wife. His children were scattered about England, and he could barely communicate. He was helpless. Little is recorded of this time. He simply lay still in his bed. And prayed. And waited for God.

13

Expanding His Coasts

Taylor could not know it at the time, but God was far from finished with His servant.

During the months in England, his second wife, Jennie, played an important role in nursing him back to a semblance of health. The two of them would be separated for long periods in the future as Jennie Taylor was needed in England and Hudson Taylor was needed in China. Still, she remained a source of strength and support for him.

When Hudson was healed of his paralysis and was healthy enough to return to China, the first thing he did was head back to the interior city of Hankow, which was on the mighty Yangtze River. Again the immensity of the unreached was impressed on him.

While there, he and a close missionary friend, C.H. Judd, officially opened the western district of the China Inland Mission. It was to be Judd's responsibility. As the work was being done, these men prayed specifically for eighteen pioneer missionaries for the provinces beyond Hankow.

In 1875 a little paper called "An Appeal for Prayer" began showing up in Christian circles and publications. It set forth Hudson Taylor's requests regarding the nine heathen provinces of western China. True to form, he was not asking for workers or for money. He was asking for prayer to almighty God. He would let the Lord work in the hearts of men and women regarding going to China or helping with the costs. He merely laid out the case and asked for prayer.

The pamphlet set the stage for God's answer to the prayer for eighteen pioneering missionaries, and much more. After taking Taylor low, God was now raising him up for His purposes. The testing had made him mature and complete and a ready vessel for the leading of the Lord.

Not coincidentally, events were falling into place in China.

All these years, Taylor and the China Inland Mission missionaries had been skirting local laws to push the gospel inland. But now the door inland was being thrown wide open for the first time in history.

The Chefoo Convention was a treaty between the British and the Imperial Chinese government in 1876. It ended the sporadic fighting between the countries and opened the closed Chinese interior to the western world. No longer would the most populous country in the world be sealed off to foreigners. The British and other countries wanted the opening for trade: more trade meant more profits. The Chinese also wanted the opening for trade, because more trade meant more goods. Furthermore, their government simply could not defeat the British in war.

But what the British meant for financial gain, God meant for souls. All of China was now an open avenue for missionaries of Jesus Christ. And no one was more ready to push the gospel through to the uttermost parts of the country than Hudson Taylor and his colleagues.

Time and again, his complete trust in God encouraged those around him as the opportunities and dangers unfolded.

A young missionary named George Nicoll had just been forced from his mission station because of rioting and had returned to Hankow to confer with Taylor. While he was conversing with him, Taylor received letters from two other stations reporting rioting and danger. It was a heavy moment, as it appeared there was a movement of opposition to the spreading of the work:

Figuring that Taylor would want to be alone, young Nicoll was about to leave the room when he heard whistling. He turned and saw Taylor softly whistling a favorite hymn:

Jesus, I am resting, resting
In the joy of what Thou art . . .

"How can you whistle when our friends are in such danger!" he burst out.

Taylor smiled patiently and gave an answer Nicoll would long remember. "Would you have me anxious and troubled? That would not help them, and would certainly cripple my work. I have just to roll the burden on the Lord."

Hudson Taylor had learned hard lessons about trusting God and rolling all his burdens on the Lord—and he had learned them well. He did not worry. He trusted God. During all this time he continued to struggle with poor health, sometimes conducting the affairs of the mission from his bed for weeks at a time.

At this time, in 1875, the China Inland Mission had grown to seventy full-time workers at twenty-eight stations—roughly half Chinese evangelists and half missionaries. There were about six hundred converts worshiping regularly. Those numbers were about to change dramatically in coming years as Taylor took full advantage of the opening provided for evangelism.

On a visit back to England in 1877, Taylor was invited to Ireland by evangelist Grattan Guinness. There, Taylor addressed a class of young men. It included Thomas Barnardo, who would go on to become known as the "Father to Nobody's Children" because of the orphanages he opened in London's poorest sections. Also in that class were three young men who would later become pioneers in the expanding scope of the China Inland Mission.

On this trip back home, Taylor prayed specifically for thirty missionaries to start evangelizing the vast western provinces. The prayers were answered as more and more missionaries responded to the call.

Taylor frequently told friends, "We want workers, not loafers." And he set the example with his unceasing work in making the case for the needs of China—when his health permitted.

Though at times he was bedridden with sickness, others were healthy and strong and ready to use their strength. John McCarthy, one of the young men Taylor had spoken to in Ireland, was now a China Inland Mission missionary. He set out to walk across China, from the Yangtze River to the Irrawaddy River in Burma, which he did in seven months. He passed out tracts and preached—and mostly showed that the whole field was ripe.

The number of missionaries who were part of the China Inland Mission had been growing steadily. But now the growth really began to take off as God was calling even more workers to the field. Looking back, the huge growth in the mission becomes evident.

In 1881, while traveling through the western provinces of China, he was led to pray for seventy more missionaries, even though there were only one hundred at the time. He continued to step out in faith that these prayers would be answered, and they were every time.

God was not only working His will, He was showing His mercy. That same year, Taylor's old-est son, Howard, was called to China as a mis-sionary and started his own missionary station. After all of the personal heartache in his family, Taylor was now able to see joyful fruit on earth.

By 1886 there were 187 China Inland Mission missionaries, and Taylor prayed for one hundred more in the next year. He also prayed for ten thousand English pounds of additional income, which would be required to support these missionaries. One year later, the last of more than one hundred new missionaries were on the voyage from Europe to China. And the entire ten thousand pounds was already provided—by just eleven donors.

As a result of this divinely provided growth, there was also the need for tremendous financial giving. Each missionary required support. Taylor never altered his tactic; only the amount was changed. Instead of asking God for one hundred English pounds for support for him and a few others, he was now asking for ten thousand or twenty thousand pounds—or more—to support hundreds. And God was providing.

The men and women who had faithfully supported the mission in the past rose to the occasion. This was particularly true of George Müller, who was supporting hundreds of orphans in his British orphanages without asking anyone for money. Like Taylor, he constantly took all of his requests to God. Müller increased his giving to the China Inland Mission considerably, and checks from him often arrived just when the money was needed.

That continued faithful reliance on God's provision would be needed time and again as the mission was about to explode.

14

To Every Creature

Mission stations were opening with ease now, as Western Christians poured into China, and the Chinese finally began to really hear the Word. The Light was penetrating the darkness.

The China Inland Mission was at the forefront of this movement, acting as the "shock troops," taking the gospel where it had never been taken before. The mission also supplied the majority of manpower for the job.

Taylor was spending more and more of his time traveling around the world, telling Christians everywhere about the needs of China. In the process he was drawing missionaries into the China Inland Mission from many countries and backgrounds. It was not evident at the time, but Taylor's influence was widening, as was the appeal of the mission.

On a trip to Sweden about this time, he had a new understanding of the scriptural command to take the gospel to "every creature." He wrote:

> I confess with shame that until that moment the question of what our Lord really meant by His command "Preach the gospel to every creature" had never been raised by me. I had labored for many years, as have many others, to carry the gospel farther afield—had laid plans for reaching every unreached province and many smaller districts in China—without realizing the plain meaning of our Savior's words!

He figured there were about forty thousand active Protestant believers in China. If that number were tripled to include every Christian possible, and if every one became a messenger to eight of his countrymen, that would still total less than one million Chinese reached by the gospel. But there were hundreds of millions of Chinese!

The words "to every creature" burned in his soul. For all of his remarkable actions, he had not seen them literally enough. He feared he had not obeyed them. He now wrestled with these words of Jesus at the home of a Swedish pastor.

"How are we going to trust the Lord Jesus Christ with reference to this command?" Taylor asked. He had been pondering the command in his heart for days, the burden growing as a new understanding revealed itself.

"Ought we to completely drop the title Lord as applied to Him and simply recognize Him as Savior so far as the penalty of our sin is concerned? Are we, in fact, unprepared to agree that we have been 'bought with a price'—that we are owned—and that He has the right to unquestioning obedience? Or is it that we are willing to agree that something may perhaps be due Him, but only as long as it is not too costly—as long, that is, as Jesus does not demand too much sacrifice?"

He paced the room, the wood floor creaking beneath his old shoes, and stroked his long, graying beard. The very idea of not obeying Christ pained Taylor.

"Surely, Brother, you have been obedient," the Swede said. "Look how God has blessed your work in China."

Taylor stopped and stared at him. His eyes were alive and intense behind his small eyeglasses. He seemed to look right at the man without seeing him. He was in no mood to rest on what he had accomplished so far.

"How few of us have ever really realized that Christ is either Lord of all or He is not Lord at all!"

The statement burned into the pastor's heart, as it would for any Christian. To obey every command of Christ—this was an awesome idea to think about actually putting into practice. And now a man who was in the midst of taking the gospel to thousands—maybe millions, eventually—was being convicted in his spirit about not obeying the command to take the Word "to every creature."

"Mr. Taylor, you have done such a marvelous work in China. No man can really obey to the maximum every command God has laid down. After all, His Word tells us we are weak in the flesh."

Taylor would have none of it. He turned back from the window, hands clasped behind his back.

"There are no excuses for disobedience! If we can judge God's Word as much or as little as we like, then we are lords, and He is indebted to us for whatever we choose to obey. If, on the other hand, He is Lord, let us treat Him as such."

He stopped as the pastor looked down at his Bible. Then Taylor continued:

"Jesus knew. 'Why do you call Me, "Lord, Lord," and do not do the things which I say?'"

Taylor had another ten years of active service ahead for the mission, and it was to be focused on this point. He was about to enter into the widest possible view of God's calling on his life—a scale he could never have imagined as a sickly teenager living on apples and bread in London.

The command to take Jesus to every creature was now alive in his heart, and he put feet to it. It was as if the order had just been given, and it was urgent that it be carried out. Now that he understood that God would provide all that was necessary to carry out His will, Taylor was not worried. It was a divine command that did not rely only on his own actions. He just needed to do his part faithfully.

"Even if we begin at once, millions will have passed away before we can reach them," he realized.

What, actually, was he to begin? Taking the word of the gospel to every man, woman and child in China was the obvious and awesome answer. He did not consider if it should be attempted, merely how to go about it. The order was already given and was to be obeyed.

So he wrote down a mathematical equation. One million is a thousand thousands. With one thousand evangelists, each one teaching the gospel to two hundred and fifty people daily, two hundred and fifty million people could be reached in one thousand days. With these assumptions most of China could be reached in three to four years!

Now Hudson Taylor knew very well that many objections could be raised to the calculation. The biggest would be for each person to reach two hundred and fifty people per day—new people, no less. But he remembered the fruit of his early evangelistic work, particularly when traveling with William Burns. They frequently reached five hundred to one thousand people in a day, telling people of Christ where no missionaries had gone. It could be done.

He did not need to concern himself with taking the time to "talk" each Chinese into belief. His duty was merely to carry the word to every Chinese. To convict the heart was the work of the Holy Spirit, and then each individual soul could choose salvation or not.

Also, he figured, growth in the Christian walk, the next step, would come through maturing Christians in the country and, ultimately of course, from the Lord.

So in 1890 Taylor again felt at liberty to pray for a specific number of missionaries—this time, one thousand over five years. Like the other prayers, it was a huge step of faith. There were then fewer than five hundred missionaries in the China Inland Mission.

In the December issue of *China's Millions*, a little publication of the China Inland Mission, there was an article entitled, "To Every Creature." It was a plea for immediate action on behalf of every Chinese. It first sought help in the realm where every believer has power—prayer. It next sought a united front from all missionary societies to field one thousand workers, because Taylor did not think that the China Inland Mission alone could do it.

His vision was growing and sharpening. He traveled back to China for the General Missionary Conference of 1890, grateful for the opportunity to lay the issue before the faithful missionaries who were in the field.

"We cannot take hold of this thing in earnest without getting more than one thousand. Oh, the enlargement, the enrichment that would come in the train of such a movement! Could China be blessed alone? Would not the whole world necessarily share in the blessing!"

His heart overflowed as he spoke to the gathering of leading missionaries—men and women who yearned for what he yearned for, an opportunity of salvation for all the Chinese.

"I do not know that we are told anywhere in the Bible to try to do anything. 'We must try to do the best we can' is a very common expression; but I remember some years ago, after hearing a remark of that kind, looking carefully through the New Testament to see under what circumstances the disciples were told to try to do anything. I was surprised not to find any."

He then did the same with the Old Testament, with the same result.

"There were many commands that appeared impossible to obey, but they were definite commands; and I think we all need to set ourselves, not to try to obey our Lord as far as we can, but simply to obey Him!"

Taylor was now on fire.

"If, as an organized Conference, we were to set ourselves to obey the command of the Lord to the fullest—if, as an act of obedience, we were to determine that every district, every town, every village, every hamlet in this land should hear the gospel, and were to set about doing it—I believe that the Spirit would come down in such mighty power that we would find supplies springing up we know not how. We would find the fire spreading from missionary to flock, and our Chinese fellow-workers and the whole Church of God would be blessed!"

He brought the focus back to simple, complete obedience: "God gives His Holy Spirit to those who obey Him."

God's hand was busily at work around the globe even as Taylor spoke. A group of four

Australian Christians were convicted separately about the need to reach the Chinese. God brought them together and then into touch with the China Inland Mission. Similar convictions of the heart were reported in Canada, Scandinavia, Tasmania, England, Germany and the USA.

Taylor's heart was opened now beyond China. As he traveled to different countries, he made plain the need for the gospel everywhere it was not adequately preached: in India, South America, the Philippines—everywhere. He was aware that a soul without the knowledge of Christ was a terrible thing, wherever the person lived on earth.

By the time accounts were tallied at the end of 1895, five years after the prayer and the appeal was first made, 1,153 new missionaries were laboring for the Lord as part of the China Inland Mission.

And while that brought an immense strain on resources—from training to counseling to supplies—Taylor refused to budge from what he felt was a God-ordained method of handling the money. There would be no borrowing, no debt. God would supply all that was needed. And if He did not, then it was not needed.

Taylor's ever-deepening faith encouraged those around him as he proved on a daily basis that God is indeed faithful.

For instance, there was a day in 1891 when there was urgent need for two thousand English pounds to cover expenses. A cable transferring funds arrived, and everyone at the China headquarters waited as a young man, who was training to be a missionary, read the amount.

"One hundred and seventy pounds," he read slowly.

"Wait," another said, "that must be a mistake!"

Another ventured, "Perhaps it should be one thousand and seven hundred pounds."

"No, it clearly reads one hundred and seventy pounds."

That was indeed the amount. And it was well short of what was required. One of the young missionaries turned to Taylor, who was seated on a wooden chair at his small desk.

"But we need two thousand pounds, Mr. Taylor."

He, of course, knew that; and he knew from experience that they would need much more because, with about five hundred missionaries in the field, unexpected expenses always came up.

"Sir, this is the last cable for a month," another man said in desperation. "We won't have enough money."

For a moment there was a feeling of panic among those present. But Taylor turned in his chair and smiled calmly at the tense group. With a hint of joy in his voice, he gave a classic reply concerning living by faith—one that none in that room ever forgot:

"Now you will watch and see what God will do!"

Taylor saw this as nothing more than an opportunity for God to show His power and authority, and for the young men to learn to trust God.

And, of course, God showed Himself faithful. By a combination of unusual circumstances, including an unusually large gift from Chinese Christians, every expense for the month, including the known two thousand pounds, was covered. There was even a little money left over.

By the turn of the nineteenth century, the China Inland Mission was providing more than half of all missionaries in China—more than all other mission societies and denominations combined.

Taylor had opened his mouth wide—just as Berger, years earlier, had counseled him to do. And God had truly filled it!

15

Storm Clouds Burst

The opening of China had been a grand blessing for spreading the Word. Many workers were being called to the harvest.

But a backlash was building up among segments of the Chinese population, and anti-foreign feelings were reaching a fever pitch. Breaking down China's centuries of seclusion was not going to be easy or smooth. The Imperial Chinese government in Peking was faltering. It had been weakened by corruption and a poor reputation, and it now even backed some of the anti-foreign rebels. As the iron grip of government loosened, this released forces of disarray in many parts of the country. Sporadic riots and disorder in the cities resulted.

Before full-scale rebellion broke out in China, there occurred a Muslim Rebellion in the mountainous province of Tsinghai.

In that far northwestern province, the Muslims—followers of the prophet Muhammad—were a sizable minority. The only missionaries operating that far into the interior were from the China Inland Mission, and their stations were all threatened as the Muslim rebels attacked cities and fought the government's troops.

One particular case involved missionaries at Sining, the province's capital. No one outside the area knew of the peril they were in as ten thousand Muslim troops suddenly swept out of the surrounding mountains and besieged the city. As the battle unfolded, wounded Chinese soldiers and civilians fled into the city. Mr. and Mrs. Ridley and J.C. Hall, the China Inland Mission missionaries, worked feverishly to care for the wounded. They also treated hundreds of women and children who had escaped slaughter in the countryside and were huddled in a temple.

The missionaries could have left the city when they had the chance before the Muslims attacked. But they chose to stay. Years of preaching had converted only a few people, but the opportunity to sacrifice themselves to help the Chinese provided a powerful picture of the gospel in action. For seven months they labored with thousands of the wounded, risking their lives regularly. Then, when the Chinese finally beat off the enemy, the missionaries cared also for the Muslims, who were suffering terrible revenge.

During this long trial no money, letters or help of any kind could get through to the Ridleys and Hall. Taylor was intensely involved with trying to get help in, but nothing was possible. He could only roll his concern onto his heavenly Father.

After nearly two years and the deaths of eighty thousand people, the uprising was quashed and peace returned. The missionaries had proved themselves friends to both the Chinese and the Muslims, and now they had a ministry of unequaled authority in the region. Wherever they went, they were welcomed with open arms and Christ was made known.

However, about this same time Japan defeated China in a war and in 1895 took over the area in the northeast known as Manchuria. That, combined with the growing number of foreigners (including Christian missionaries) living in China, stirred up feelings against all foreigners. Many Chinese feared their country was being taken advantage of and began forming groups to take action against it.

The core group was a secret Chinese society of patriots known as the "Society of Harmonious Fists." Foreigners referred to the group as the "Boxers." The Boxers were nationalists who wanted to return China to its tradition of being separate from the rest of the world. Their main targets were the Imperial Manchu leaders, all foreigners and Chinese Christians. Their stated goal was to kill every single person who fell into any of those groups—and they made every effort to do just that.

The first hint of problems for missionaries came as early as 1895 when Robert Stewart, a member of the Church Missionary Society, his wife, his children and eight Chinese co-workers, were brutally murdered in the city of their ministry. It was like a lightning bolt preceding the storm.

Taylor foresaw the growing threat. He understood the Chinese people, so he wrote friends and other missionaries about the impending danger. But there was nothing to do but leave matters in God's hands.

In late 1899 William Fleming of Australia became the first China Inland Missionary to be martyred. He was killed trying to protect his Chinese helper, P'an, a convert from the Black Meo tribe to whom he was ministering. The attack was part of the anti-Christian hysteria. Both men were killed.

Taylor took the news hard and feared what it meant.

"How sad the tidings! It is blessed for the

martyrs, but sad for us, for their friends, and for China. And not only sad, but threatening! It seems to show that God is about to test us with a new kind of trial. Doubtless it means a fuller blessing—but through a deeper suffering."

It would indeed involve deep suffering.

In 1900 events in China escalated rapidly. The spreading revolt soon blew into a full-scale, brutal revolution that became known to the world as the Boxer Rebellion. It was a savage uprising.

Because the China Inland Mission had been so successful in penetrating China and sending out workers into the harvest, they also suffered the most. The small missionary stations and their converts were completely vulnerable to the marauding Boxer rebels—and to others who just wanted to steal and destroy.

When the rebellion exploded, Taylor was out of China, traveling in the United States and England. He was unable to go to China because of his health, but he knew that there needed to be local control of the mission there. He appointed D.E. Hoste as the acting general director.

Again, as he had so often been in his life, he was almost helpless as reports of the carnage poured in to him from Asia.

On June 1, right before breakfast, he received a startling telegram: Riot in Chengtu (capital of Szechwan province). All missions destroyed. Friends in Yarnell.

Another telegram arrived telling of riots and destruction at a nearby outpost. One report after another piled in on Taylor, until within just ten days he had been informed of the destruction of every mission but one in the entire Szechwan province. The rioting and attacks on Chinese Christians had forced many of them to flee to the mission compounds for safety. But there was no safety there. It began to look as though all of the work that been done over the years was being undone. Now the doubts crept in.

Could it all have been for nothing? Will God not put a stop to it?

As the rebellion spread to every province, the violence increased. New reports of murdered missionaries began reaching Taylor.

He read every report with tears flowing freely. One report came in about two missionary women who had been brutally killed by a large gang of Chinese. He could have questioned his decision about sending in single women. Or he could have raged against the unfairness of it. Instead, Taylor choked out through the tears, "Oh, think what it must have been to exchange that murderous mob for the rapture of Christ's presence—His bosom, His smile."

The reports kept coming in—more and more filled with accounts of deaths—until Taylor was ready to break, unable to take any more of the tragic news. Having reached the bottom, he said, "I cannot read, I cannot think, I cannot even pray."

There was one thing he could always do: "But I can trust."

The Boxers took over much of the central government in Peking and administrative seats in other parts of the country. They made good on their promises and tried to kill every foreigner and professing Chinese Christian they could find. They surrounded the foreign embassies in Peking, refusing to let anyone go in or leave, and they murdered the German and Japanese ambassadors.

These violent actions brought in foreign troops to protect their respective citizens and help the Chinese government. Soldiers came from the United States, Russia, Germany, Japan, Great Britain, Italy, Austria and France. These troops helped the government to put down the rebellion and, by September 1901, to restore peace. When it was all over, the Chinese government agreed to pay $330 million to the foreign powers for their intervention—but most of it was never paid, or, as in the case of the United States, it was returned.

The rebellion had been brief but so bloody!

Missionaries and foreigners had suffered throughout the country. But the China Inland Mission suffered the worst: fifty-eight missionaries had been murdered during the rebellion. Another twenty-one children of missionaries were killed or died. And hundreds, maybe thousands, of Chinese Christians were slaughtered.

It was a deep price to pay for taking the gospel into the country. But it was a price that every missionary had realized was a real possibility. And it bought forth an even greater blessing.

16

Finishing the Race Strong

Hudson Taylor felt a certain earthly responsibility regarding the missionaries of the China Inland Mission who had been killed during the Boxer Rebellion. But he continued to trust only in God and keep his eyes focused on soul-winning.

Although it was offered, Taylor steadfastly refused any remuneration for the property and buildings that had been destroyed in the rebellion. Some of his missionaries wanted him to accept the money, knowing the mission's usual financial difficulties. Instead, Taylor trusted in God to provide and watched for an opportunity for His power to be manifest. The decision made the love of Christ real to the Chinese and endeared the missionaries to the people.

Soon the work began to flourish again—more than it ever had.

Taylor's health continued to decline. In 1902 he resigned as general director for the China Inland Mission, handing it over to the faithful and competent D.E. Hoste. There was a huge amount of work to do, for the seed of the gospel that was sown in faith and watered with tears was bursting forth. The harvest field was ready. As Taylor had expected, the price had been steep, but the blessings were greater.

Resigning from the China Inland Mission was not easy for Hudson Taylor, who had spent his entire adult life laboring tirelessly for his Lord. His true joy was to do all for Jesus. Sacrifice and labor were both a joy when done for Jesus, he said, then added, "But it's hardest of all to do nothing for His sake."

Figuring he would never see China again, he and Jennie went to a friend's residence in Switzerland and set up a headquarters to handle the crush of correspondence he constantly received from all over the world. Jennie was nearing the end of her earthly life, and she lay bedridden for weeks in 1904 with cancer. At the end her breathing became very difficult.

"No pain, no pain," she assured her anxious husband late one evening. But he could see her troubles and stayed by her until morning. When she opened her eyes after suffering through the night, she clearly could see the anguish on Hudson's face.

"Ask Him to take me quickly," she said in a whisper.

It was a very hard prayer to offer up. But Hudson did so for her sake, asking the Lord to take this waiting soul.

Near the end, she said, "He will not fail." Within minutes her breathing became quiet, and then she slipped away into the arms of Jesus. Taylor now had to bury his second faithful wife. He was full of grief and loss and again, as always, fell back on Him who is sufficient for all our needs.

During that long, cold winter in the mountains, he was comforted by the company of his niece—the daughter of his dear sister Amelia—and some old friends who came to encourage him. His health improved substantially, surprising the doctors. So much did it improve that he decided he could try to return to China!

The arrangements were made, and shortly the frail, elderly Hudson Taylor was on his way back to China for this one time. He arrived in Shanghai in April 1905.

This last trip was full of wonderful—and sometimes poignant—memories for Hudson. Shanghai was where he had started his mission work. Traveling with his missionary son Howard and his wife, he spent Easter in Yangchow where he had lived for quite a while. This was near where he had buried Maria and the children who had died so young in China. But those thoughts now were not sad anymore because of the parting long ago. Instead, they were amazingly happy. Taylor knew he would not live much longer and that he would be reunited in Jesus with all of them.

He traveled by steamer to Hankow. This city, so full of spiritual darkness and a distrust of foreigners when Taylor first arrived there, was now a busy center of missionary activity. Missionaries and supplies passed through Hankow to hundreds of missionary stations to the west that were busy reaching thousands of Chinese. The workers faithfully proclaimed the most important thing—salvation through Jesus. But they also brought medicine to heal the sick and food to feed the hungry. Many physical needs were being cared for as the Word was spread.

Taylor could see the magnitude of the work begun so many years previously with nothing but faith. He marveled at how God had used a penniless teenager to start it all.

He decided to travel on the new railroad being extended northward and stopped at the Yengchang mission which had been opened because of the railway. So much was happening he could only shake his head in amazement! The group then made a journey overland to a brand-new mission station, a trip that involved staying overnight at a roadside inn. A touching incident happened there.

In the morning Taylor found that their stay was without charge. The cost for the room and food had been paid by a Chinese Christian who felt it was his responsibility to care for the "venerable chief pastor" while he was in his city. It was done anonymously, and neither Taylor nor his companions knew who the Chinese brother was who paid the bill. It was known, however, to the One who registers all our treasures in heaven.

Taylor also stopped at the missionary station where his daughter and her husband worked. What a joy it was to be traveling with his missionary son and daughter-in-law, visiting the mission of his daughter Maria (now Mrs. J.J. Coulthard) and son-in-law. He could see his own godly heritage in their activity for the kingdom.

As the party journeyed through the region, the Christians of town after town welcomed them and lavished Taylor with love and attention. In a couple of small towns, the people lined the streets, holding lights to welcome him; in another they put up a huge banner to welcome the venerable chief pastor. One town even created a fancy satin banner containing the scarlet-painted words: "O man greatly beloved."

Taylor was amazed at the depth of feelings for him personally among the Chinese who had put their trust in Jesus. He was a little embarrassed at all the attention.

On May 26, 1905, he arrived back in Hankow. He was now 73 years old and getting weaker by the day. The old body that had suffered frequent illness and been pushed to the limit for so many years was giving out. He met with all of the missionaries in the city over the next few days and gave some final counsel. After one meeting a missionary doctor stayed and told Taylor that he sometimes felt hindered in prayer because he thought certain things were too small to pray about. Taylor responded, "There is nothing small, and there is nothing great. In fact, only God is great, and we should trust Him fully." He didn't know anything about things too small for prayer! Even in his last days, complete trust in the Father dominated his existence.

The next evening, at his son's home in Hankow, he did not come down for dinner.

His daughter-in-law, who referred to him lovingly as her "dear father," checked on him. She found him in bed, leaning over some letters. She positioned things comfortably and sat down next to him. She gives this description of those final moments on June 3, 1905:

"I was just in the middle of a sentence when father turned his head quickly and gave a little gasp. I looked up, thinking he was going to sneeze. But another gasp came, and another! He gave no cry and said no word. He was not choking or distressed for breath. I cannot call it death—but a glad, swift entry into life immortal.

"Oh, the look of rest and calm that came over his dear face! It was wonderful. The weight of the years seemed to pass away in a few moments. The weary lines vanished. He looked like a child quietly sleeping, and the very room seemed full of unutterable peace."

In that moment the gates of heaven swung open and the angels rejoiced as a saint of the Lord crossed the river and entered into the presence of the Savior who was Lord of his life. A mighty warrior, though a frail man, this everlasting soul had arrived Home. And because of his faithful labors for Jesus, heaven was a fuller place.